www.brookscole.com

www.brookscole.com is the World Wide Web site for Thomson Brooks/Cole and is your direct source to dozens of online resources.

At *www.brookscole.com* you can find out about supplements, demonstration software, and student resources. You can also send email to many of our authors and preview new publications and exciting new technologies.

www.brookscole.com
Changing the way the world learns®

Group Work Activities
in Generalist Practice

Diane C. Haslett
University of Maine, Orono

THOMSON

BROOKS/COLE

Australia • Canada • Mexico • Singapore • Spain • United Kingdom • United States

Executive Editor: *Lisa Gebo*
Assistant Editor: *Alma Dea Michelena*
Editorial Assistant: *Sheila Walsh*
Technology Project Manager: *Barry Connolly*
Marketing Manager: *Caroline Conchilla*
Marketing Assistant: *Mary Ho*
Advertising Project Manager: *Tami Strang*

Project Manager, Editorial Production:
Christy Krueger
Print Buyer: *Emma Claydon*
Permissions Editor: *Stephanie Lee*
Cover Designer: *Ross Carron*
Compositor: *Hoby Corp.*
Proofreader: *Barbara Markowitz*
Printer: *Thomson West*

For more information about our products,
contact us at:
Thomson Learning Academic Resource Center
1-800-423-0563

For permission to use material from this text or
product, submit a request online at
http://www.thomsonrights.com
Any additional questions about permissions can be
submitted by email at
thomsonrights@thomson.com

Library of Congress Control Number: 2004105612

ISBN: 0-534-61785-9

Thomson Brooks/Cole
10 Davis Drive
Belmont, CA 94002-3098
USA

Asia
Thomson Learning
5 Shenton Way #01-01
UIC Building
Singapore 068808

Australia/New Zealand
Thomson Learning
102 Dodds Street
Southbank, Victoria 3006
Australia

Canada
Nelson
1120 Birchmount Road
Toronto, Ontario M1K 5G4
Canada

Europe/Middle East/South Africa
Thomson Learning
High Holborn House
50/51 Bedford Row
London WC1R 4LR
United Kingdom

Latin America
Thomson Learning
Seneca, 53
Colonia Polanco
11560 Mexico D.F.
Mexico

Spain/Portugal
Paraninfo
Calle/Magallanes, 25
28015 Madrid, Spain

Table of Contents

PREFACE

Purpose: Since the move to generalist practice in schools of social work, group workers, both educators and practitioners alike, have been alarmed at the apparent decreased emphasis on group work in the practice curriculum. Students have also asked why more hands-on content for working with groups is not available. The aim of this manual is to supply access to this material to two primary audiences: 1. students and instructors, and 2. group workers currently in practice in a variety of social service settings. The manual provides activities for classroom experiences that teach skillful use of the full range of activities, both action-oriented and verbal, as a central component of competent generalist practice with groups. These activities demonstrate the parallel process between the experience in the classroom and future application in the practice setting, a cornerstone of social work education. Moreover, those using this manual will gain a clearer understanding of and exposure to the ways that both action-oriented and verbal activities bring a powerful dimension to work with groups.

Approach: In the classroom setting, the manual is designed primarily for use by students in socio-educational task groups as a supplement to a basic text on generalist practice chosen by the instructor. It can also perform a similar function in conjunction with courses specific to social work practice with groups. In the field, the manual can stand alone, with the group worker supplying supplementary readings to group members as needed. The emphasis in each circumstance, in the classroom or in the agency, is on understanding and applying activities in the group, grounding the application in relevant theory and practice with groups. Action-oriented activities that provide use of the broad range of group members' senses (e.g., visual, auditory, kinesthetic) have a central place in this manual and employ a range of media such as art, photography, movement, and poetry. More traditional verbal activities (i.e., discussion, paper/pencil exercises) are included as well. This focus enlarges the student's repertoire and reinforces the notion that social workers work with the whole person. Attention is given to activities suitable for both agency-based task and treatment groups. Finally, the implications of using activities with diverse groups and group members are discussed in each set of activity instructions under the component, *In the Field*, where those issues are particularly relevant.

Activities are set in the context of stages of group development. Most texts discussing groups cover various models of group development. This manual uses the five-part Boston Model developed by Garland, Jones, and Kolodny found in Bernstein's (1973) *Explorations in group work: Essays in theory and practice* (pp. 17-71)—preaffiliation, power and control, intimacy, differentiation, separation. Workers have observed that some groups may not proceed through all the stages in an orderly and sequential manner or complete the stages in an altered order. For example, groups with high turnover in members (e.g., psychoeducational groups in hospitals) may stay in the earlier stages. Workers with women's therapy groups have noted that these groups often change the stage sequence. Schiller (1995) has recast the Boston Model based on her work with women's group—preaffiliation, establishing a relational base, mutuality and interpersonal empathy, challenge and change, separation. However, for our purposes here the Boston Model provides a firm grounding for students in mixed socio-educational groups who are beginning to make sense of what they are experiencing with groups both in class and in the field. Where a group worker might use the activity in more than one stage of group development, the suggested adaptations are included under *In the Field* in the description of the activity as it might be used in agency practice. Once students have participated in an activity, they can add it to their resources for possible future use in their field placements or later professional practice, making the necessary adaptations to the needs of the groups with whom they work. The component *Practitioner's Notes* helps guide students as they transfer their learning from the classroom to the field

Coverage: The manual has two major sections: Activities and the Resource Bibliography. The Activities have three sources: original work by the author, adapted work from other sources, and work contributed by colleagues. The Activities chapters presents detailed instructions for action-oriented and verbal group activities divided into five sections linked to content usually covered in generalist practice courses:

- Beginnings with Groups in Generalist Practice,
- Introducing Theory and Skills for Generalist Practice with Groups,
- Interventions in Middle Stages of Group Development,
- Supervision and In-service Training,
- Endings Activities for Groups in Generalist Practice.

The format for each activity includes:

- the goal for use in the classroom setting,
- the parallel use in the field,
- the number of participants that can engage usefully in the activity,
- the materials and equipment needed and, in some cases, sources for purchasing necessary equipment,
- the estimated time the activity requires,
- the space required for the activity to be accomplished comfortably,
- the preparation participants need to make before the activity will take place,
- instructions for each aspect of the activity,
- a space for the student to keep notes for using activity in the practice setting,
- the source of the activity if it is not original with the author of the manual.

In many instances, instruction sheets and other print materials needed for the activity follow the instructions. Instructors and group facilitators may wish participants to use these forms directly in the manual. They may also duplicate the forms directly for use with their classes or groups or adapt them to the needs of their particular situation. The Resource Bibliography contains a list of relevant web sites, texts, and journal articles. It also includes a list of suppliers of equipment and materials for a wide range of activities. These resources will support group workers in selecting activities for use in their various groups and to encourage further research and development of new approaches by faculty, students, and social work practitioners. These lists are not exhaustive but give faculty, trainers, practitioners, and students a starting point in developing their own activities library. Many items listed are available in public and/or university libraries and can be ordered through inter-library loan quite easily. Bookstores and on-line sources for book bargains are also excellent sources for building an activities library. The Bibliography owes its length and breadth to colleagues who have shared their enthusiasm for using program activities with their groups in practice and in the classroom and to students who have been generous in contributing their time and their "finds" as part of their class work, in independent studies, and from their discoveries in their field placements.

References:

Garland, J.A., Jones, H.E., Kolodny, R.L. (1973). A model for stages of group development in social work groups (pp. 17-71). In S. Bernstein (Ed.). *Explorations in group work: Essays in theory and practice.* Boston: Milford House, Inc.

Schiller, L.Y. (1995). Stages of development in women's groups: A relational model (pp.117-138). In R. Kurland and R. Salmon (Eds.). *Group work practice in a troubled society: Problems and opportunities.* New York: Haworth Press.

ACKNOWLEDGEMENTS

A project like this book cannot be created in isolation. Many of my colleagues, students, and friends in both the academic and practice communities contributed to the process and were remarkably generous with their time, support, and helpful comments along the way. They have also been generous in sharing their work, as the credits on several of the activities attest. I am immensely grateful for all that they have given to me and to this effort. In particular I would like to thank Elaine Finnegan, first my MSW field instructor and now my friend, who helped me learn the basics, then the fine points of group work, and has always had just the right piece of information at just the right time. John Ramey, former General Secretary of the Association for the Advancement of Social Work with Groups, was especially helpful with his vast knowledge of group work history, both formal and informal, and is always just an email click away. My readers here in Maine, Susan Buzzell and Jane Harris-Bartley spent hours reading the manuscript in its early stages and offered many helpful comments and corrections. I would also like to thank these additional reviewers for their input: Joanne Gumpert, Marywood University; Donna Hurdle, Arizona State University and Steven Rose, Louisiana State University.

None of this effort would have been possible without the support of the University of Maine School of Social Work—Gail Werrbach, Director, Nancy Kelly, Field Coordinator, and Sandy Butler, colleague extraordinaire—and the Sabbatical semester that the University provided. The manuscript would never even have been envisioned without Lisa Gebo, Executive Editor for Brooks/Cole, who first suggested the idea several years ago at the Baccalaureate Program Directors Meeting in San Francisco and was persistent in the belief that such a project was possible. It would not have reached its current stage without the work of Alma Dea Michelena, Assistant Editor for Social Work at Brooks/Cole, who answered questions, supplied reference books on a moment's notice, and was unfailingly good natured throughout. Finally, I would like to thank my husband, Jerry Haslett, who survived the ups and downs of this adventure with me.

I hear, and I forget.

I see, and I remember.

I do, and I understand.

Confucius

INTRODUCTION

Social work practice with groups is rooted in settlement houses and other organizations, such as the Jewish Community Centers, the YM/YWCAs, and other character-building organizations for children and teens, that emerged in the Progressive Era (Middleman, 1962). For example, Jane Addams and her colleagues at Hull House created a vast array of programs to meet the needs of recent immigrants, young and old, living on Chicago's Near West Side. Miss Addams and the Hull House residents had skills in the arts, crafts, physical education, and other practical activities to share with their neighbors in the West Side community, many of whom brought similar skills from their homelands. The programs engaged groups of children, teens, and adults in doing things together—sewing doll clothes, creating pottery, cooking, weaving, doing gymnastics, or acting in the Little Theatre. The relationships that developed between the worker and the group members and among the group members happened in the context of doing these activities. Members and workers also gave and received help with the problems of daily living in the context of the activities. The continued existence of similar programs in the agencies under the umbrella of today's Hull House Association and other social agencies nationally makes a strong argument for the usefulness and resiliency of this approach to social services.

As the practice of group work grew and changed in the first half of the twentieth century, group workers faced the dilemma of finding a professional home. Were they part of the emerging profession of social work or were they more akin to recreation and education? As group workers made the decision to join with social work and as social work focused more on talking therapies, group workers developed practice approaches that would align group work more fully with the mainstream of the social work profession. Less and less emphasis was placed on "doing," usually identified in the group worker's lexicon as program activities, "a term used to describe the activities…. such as the expressive arts (e.g., painting, dancing), games, folk singing, social parties cooking—in fact, almost any recreational or social activity used by people in groups" (Shulman, 1999, p. 632). The very essence of the group work method and the element that had been its forte historically largely disappeared. The course content on program activities in professional social work education followed suit. Full courses on program activities (e.g., group singing, arts and crafts, folk dancing) were eliminated from the curriculum (Ramey, 2002, private communication) and discussion of program activities was restricted to a class lecture or two (Kurland and Salmon, 1998; Middleman, 1962).

Since the advent of generalist practice in the 1960s, most BSW and MSW programs have reduced the presence of required courses in group work and virtually eliminated content on program activities as an approach to work with client populations in generalist practice courses (Birnbaum & Wayne, 2000; Knight, 2001). Given the scope of the coverage required in texts on generalist practice, the topic of program activities in group work receives scant coverage. Although some group work texts retain content on program activities (Brandler & Roman, 1991; Doel & Sawdon, 1999; Henry, 1992; Shulman, 1992; Sundel, Glasser, Sarri, & Vinter, 1985; Toseland & Rivas, 2001), generalist practice texts have little material on the topic. None of the texts begins to cover these approaches with the depth found in earlier books on group work. For example, Wilson and Ryland's (1949) *Social Group Work Practice* devoted more than one-third of their text to an "analysis of program media" (pp. 197-303) and included practice examples with strong program media content in the remaining chapters. Meanwhile students in field practice are expected to work effectively with diverse populations in their practice with small groups, and their supervisors often suggest that they use an activity focus with these groups much to the dismay of the field intern (Wright, 2003).

This gap between the preparation in the classroom and the expectations in the agency has profound consequences for the student social worker and as well as those who seek social work services. Students' development of requisite skills for practice that is truly generalist is truncated. Furthermore, clients who may prefer more action-oriented assistance and whole client populations who are unable or unprepared to benefit from more verbal means of assessment and intervention are shortchanged when the social worker is unprepared to select and implement program activities in the groups they serve. This manual seeks to reunite the "talking" and the "doing" in what Shulman calls "a mixed transactional model" where the group worker and members work together on carefully selected activities in either task or treatment groups (Shulman, 1999, p. 632). Systematic use of activities integrated into the weekly classroom experience offers students immediate exposure to the use of program activities in group work and a platform from which to apply these skills with their groups in field placements and in future professional practice. Students become well-rounded, competent practitioners ready and able to apply skills that are, in fact, generalist in the fullest sense. Ultimately, the people with whom these students work benefit from an approach that honors the whole human being—thinking, feeling, acting—with a full range of skills to address group members' presenting issues.

Using this Manual - A Note to Students: As you begin your social work education, you may be hesitant to try your hand at working with groups. The activities in this manual are designed to help you learn one of the principal ways social workers and group members work together to achieve both individual and group goals. In your role as a beginning social worker practicing with groups, you will learn that activities are a powerful intervention tool, not time fillers or mere entertainment for the group. You will consider carefully all the variables that make one activity a better choice for a particular group at a particular stage of group development. Each activity in the manual gives specific instructions on what is needed for the preparation and implementation of the activity and encourages you to look beyond the written instructions to adapt and develop your own approach to using activities with your groups. To assist you in selecting activities for use in your groups, a series of four classifications is included in the *Appendixes*. The activities are classified by type of activity (e.g., arts and crafts, music, movement), by suitability at each of the five stages of group development (preaffiliation, power and control, intimacy, differentiation, separation), and by applicability for either task or treatment groups.

In the Classroom: Each of the chapters covers material linked to topics you will be studying. Your instructor will select particular activities to help reinforce the assigned readings and to give you an opportunity to put what you are studying into practice in the classroom. While you are engaged in doing the activities with your classmates, you should sharpen your skills as a participant observer, noting how the activity evolves, what roles each group member assumes, what effect(s) the activity has on the group, and what the outcomes are for each group member and for the group as a whole. As you consider your participation in the activity, you should also consider how you might use this activity in your field placement. At what stage of group development and for what purpose(s) might you use this activity? What might be contraindications or pitfalls? What would you need to avoid potential pitfalls and to adapt the activity for the group(s) with whom you are working? The parallel process between what you are learning in the classroom and what you apply to your practice in the field is central in helping you to make the transition from social work student to a generalist social work practitioner competent in working with groups.

In the Field: Here are some principles to think about as you get ready to make the transition to working with your group(s) in the field. These general guidelines for selecting and implementing activities will help make your role as group worker easier to manage. You will find that the material you studied in Human Behavior and the Social Environment will be very helpful in thinking about the members of the group and assessing their skills, abilities, strengths, and areas for growth. Knowing your own skills, abilities, and interests will also help you to choose activities that both you and the group will enjoy. Knowing the agency context is also important. Your assessment of the group and its members is most important. Content that you are studying on the way groups function will help you to choose activities that will assist group members to achieve their goals for the group and for themselves. Understanding group dynamics and the stages of group development will guide your selection of activities as well. As the worker, you will want to consider:

- The demographics of the group (e.g., age, sex, ethnic/racial backgrounds, socioeconomic status, previous experience as group members)
- Developmental appropriateness of the activity
- Developmental tasks for the age group
- Level of skill required by activity - frustration tolerance of group members
- Individual skills/limitations/tastes of group members
- Possible "contagion" factors (i.e., Will one member's dislike of a particular type of activity spread to the rest of the group?)
- Possible "gadgetorial seduction" (Redl, 1966) (i.e., Will members use the materials in ways unintended by the activity; for example, using finger painting with children having low impulse control?)
- Your skills/interests/limitations
- The terrain (the room/space +/-'s)
- The program's budget
- The purpose of the group
- The goal(s) of the program
- The potential rewards gained from participating in the activity
- The stage of group development
  (preaffiliation, power & control, intimacy, differentiation, separation)
- The abilities of the group members to choose/plan/implement activities as the group progresses.

To prepare for the group meeting and for the activities the group will use, here are some things to do before the session:

- ALWAYS involve the group members in the selection, planning, and implementation of group activities;
- ALWAYS try the activity BEFORE using it in the group; preferably find a person similar to group members' age/skills to help you spot potential problem areas;
- Assemble all necessary materials well in advance of the group session and check with any group members who have responsibilities for bringing key materials;
- Consider the unintended consequences of the activity - what could go wrong (e.g., Could

the equipment be used in a harmful way?);

- Plan a couple of variations/adaptations based on your assessment of and prior experience with the group;
- Have non-disruptive options for those who can't/won't participate as planned;
- ALWAYS have back-up plans in case an activity "flops";
- Consider the pros and cons of having a model/sample if doing an arts/crafts activity;
- Consider how to involve group members in implementation;
- With the group, consider displaying the activity for staff or people visiting the agency to reinforce the positive aspects of group members' participation beyond what you have done as worker in the session.

When you begin your work in the session, here are some principles for implementing activities with the group:

- Give group a brief overview of the planned activity;
- Give specific instructions clearly and in small segments; check with group members to gauge whether they understand the instructions;
- Be available to clarify instructions individually if necessary;
- Be encouraging; the activity belongs to the members;
- Focus on enjoying the experience rather than on "perfection" in the final product.

After the session is over, your work is not done. You will want to think about what happened and what you will need to do to plan for future sessions with the group. Be sure to involve the group members in your evaluation process wherever possible. Here are some things you will do to evaluate how the session went and whether the activities accomplished the objectives you and the group set out to achieve:

- Evaluate the activity with group members and with other staff to get feedback on their perceptions of how well the activity worked;
- Evaluate the activity against the criteria you have developed for this activity in relation to the group purpose and against the goals for individual group members;
- Use evaluation data to help plan future activities.

A Note to Faculty on Using this Manual in Course Development: For more than a decade, I have taught generalist social work practice courses and social work practice with groups at both the MSW and BSW levels. Typically, generalist social work practice courses have only modest content on groups and tend to emphasize verbal skills as the primary mode for service delivery. Courses on social work practice with groups usually allocate only one session to a discussion of programming and use of activities. The challenge for you as an instructor wishing to amplify this content area lies in deciding how to restructure the syllabus and the class time to incorporate material on activities and the actual use of activities in the classroom. This manual is organized around topics usually covered in generalist practice courses. Each chapter offers a range of activities designed to reinforce content the student will be reading from the assigned text(s) and supplementary journal articles. Based on the premise that material students learn in the classroom should be applicable to their practice in the field and in later employment, each activity in this manual requires students to think beyond the immediate application in the classroom to the way they can actively translate it into practice with groups in the agency setting. Taking the time to help students make that link as you discuss the completed activity with them is a critical part of the teaching/learning process.

The Syllabus: The place where you can make a first adjustment in the generalist practice syllabus can occur in the bibliography. You may wish to review current texts and choose one that gives substantial content on work with groups and add journal articles and book chapters on program and activities to the assigned readings. You may also wish to make supplementary specialized bibliographies on activities and resources for particular population groups available to the class. Colleagues in the field often have libraries devoted to their specializations and are usually willing to share these resources with interested faculty members. In classes where students are currently in the field, you may want to encourage them to add to the class's bibliographic collection by sharing resources used in their agencies. In my classes, students have contributed materials from their work with seniors' reminiscence groups, substance abuse prevention groups for youth, adventure-based programs, horticultural therapy, and dropout prevention groups at local high schools. Many appear in the Resource Bibliography of this manual.

The group work syllabus provides more latitude for concentrating on skills in programming and use of activities. Here you can select a required text emphasizing program and activities. The bibliography can be expanded to include journal articles on program activities in specialized settings and with a variety of populations. In the course description, a clear statement that students will participate in learning various types of activities during each class session sets the tone that program and nonverbal activity are essential to the group worker's expertise. Required readings and a major assignment round out the emphasis on program and activities.

Course Organization: The organization of the generalist social work practice course is less adjustable than the group work course. Given the scope of the content included in generalist practice courses, allocation of more than one session each semester to program and activities is impractical. However, you can adapt classroom role-plays and practice vignettes to widen students' horizons. You can expose students to the usefulness of activity to enhance their work with clients in various settings. For example, role-plays focusing on data-gathering skills in group work can also highlight the use of particular activities. In such a role-play, the student/worker might use cooperative games to collect the data for assessing group members' strengths, coping abilities and interpersonal skills. In my generalist practice classes, students regularly participate in one activity designed to illustrate and apply the knowledge and skills under discussion. For example, in the session where we study communication skills, students may apply this content by focusing on using empathic responses in a small group activity and role-play (see Activity 3-7).

In the group work class, it is possible to include a wider range of material on program development and activities. Max Casper (1991), who was a master at using activities with groups, has suggested starting each class with a game to enhance students' activity repertoire. This approach, expanded to include additional types of activities, has met with success with both BSW and MSW students. Besides engaging the students in the activity, you may want to provide them with written instructions for each activity. By the end of the semester they will have a small handbook that they can use in their field placements or in their later work with groups. You might also encourage students to use the format provided by these instruction sheets to record activities that they find particularly useful in their experience. You can duplicate these additional activities for class members to add to their handbook. Students who take the time to share this information with their colleagues could receive a modest reward—a few points of "extra credit" averaged in their final grade.

Beyond knowing how to choose and use activities, students need to know where to locate materials for various projects. Part of the session(s) allocated to program should include some brainstorming of places that could provide these resources. Students usually enjoy being challenged to find free or inexpensive providers of materials. Some typical suggestions include the Yellow Pages for specific products, art supply stores, merchants who will donate small amounts of materials, the local children's museum that sells remaindered items for art projects, an "alley tour" which may produce giant appliance boxes that become an assortment of make-believe structures, or the local thrift shop that can produce fantasy costumes and the basics for a multitude of crafts projects. A student records all the suggestions, and the list is duplicated for the students' activity handbook.

In any practice course you can model the use of various types of activities. Using a multimedia approach to present content can help to address students' different learning styles and focus their attention on the utility of activities. Role-play, vignettes, skits, videos, Power Point slide show, or tapes of music with lyrics relevant to particular topics provide a few ways to enhance learning opportunities. For instance, in a practice class dealing with the impact of gender of clients, you might introduce the topic with an audiotape of "Soliloquy" (see Activity 4-11). In this song from *Carousel* Bill sings about his feelings about becoming a father. The song describes Bill's view of appropriate male gender roles for the expected baby and then his coming to grips with the idea that *he* might be a *she*. Besides hearing the lyrics, listening to the changes in melody at the transition sends a powerful message about traditional societal views of males and females. At some point during the ensuing discussion, you could highlight the potential usefulness of such activities in practice situations where group members are also struggling with gender issues.

Assignments: In two-semester generalist practice courses, two major assignments help students to integrate their knowledge of the components of practice with groups. In the first semester you might assign readings and deliver lecture content on the differential use of program activities. Students could visit a group-serving agency to observe program activities and write a paper detailing their observations and giving their critique of the program's effectiveness.

In the second semester students can demonstrate their growing understanding of the linkages among stages of group development, group composition and selection of appropriate activities in a role-play assignment. For example, in a BSW program a team project works well. The objective is for students to develop skill in applying their knowledge of group process and dynamics by choosing and demonstrating an activity suitable for an assigned group at a particular stage of that group's development. Students work in teams of two to plan the activity that can be completed in the allotted 15 minutes. On the designated day, they role-play the activity with class members who have been assigned roles as group members. Students without specific roles as observers noting the use of group work skills in a format prepared by the instructor. At the conclusion of the role-play, students participate in a class discussion evaluating the successes and the areas needing improvement. Each role-play is videotaped, and students have a copy from which to do a written analysis of their individual performances.

Similarly, students in a BSW course on practice with groups might develop and role-play a 45-minute session with a group. These students would design several strategies and activities for an entire session. Students and faculty then would critique each role-play in terms of the appropriateness of the chosen activities for the assigned group and the effectiveness of the intervention strategy. Students could write an individual evaluation of their performance.

Chapter 1
Introducing Theory and Skills for Generalist Practice with Groups

USING THEORY IN GENERALIST PRACTICE

Once the class has accomplished the activities associated with the beginning of any social work practice course (e.g., introductions, review of the syllabus, setting class norms), it is important to explore the foundation on which you will build your practice knowledge, skills, and expertise. This chapter includes activities that examine aspects of generalist systems theory, practice theory, and specific elements of group work theory. In generalist practice, systems theory shapes much of the social worker's approach to assessment and intervention. Three activities in this section help you to understand and apply some of the central theoretical principles that we use in social work practice. In A 1-1 *Hypothesis Development through Arch Building* both the students who participate in the arch building process and those who act as observers in the arch building process engage actively in creating an hypothesis about human behavior in a task group. The activity helps us to focus on the ways that our individual assumptions, hypotheses, and theories about human behavior can shape our perceptions and ensuing actions in the practice setting. If your instructor chooses to have the groups build the arch nonverbally, the activity can also introduce you to notions about the power of nonverbal communication and activity in group work. If the instructor composes the groups homogeneously on some particular dimension (e.g., age, gender, specific skill set), that homogeneity may also affect the way the group functions and, by extension, the way you develop your hypothesis.

Activity 1-2 The Eco-Systems Machine offers you an interactive, auditory, visual, and kinesthetic experience with a fanciful human "machine" that grows, changes, and diminishes as participants cooperate to create it, keep it going, and then to wind it down. This activity also illustrates key concepts in eco-systems theory and underscores the power of imagination and the effects of experiencing movement in conveying ideas without the use of words. Activity 1-3 Applying Theory in Practice is a more traditional socio-educational activity. It ties together your prior learning about theories for practice with a particular social work skill, contracting with group members. You will select a situation from the ones given in the exercise and a theory that suits that situation. Then you will apply useful elements from the theory you have selected to the process of contracting with the group or individual members of the group. The end product of the activity will be the completion of the first two elements of the contract: (a) problem/issue identification and (b) goal setting linked to the identified problems or issues. Beyond the content that the activity reinforces, you will also experience the ways a group begins to work together to accomplish an assigned task. This activity opens a way for you to observe and reflect on key elements of group dynamics.

The remaining activities in this chapter cover specific aspects of social work practice with groups. Activity 1-4 *The Breakfast Club* portrays the five stages of group development and asks you to apply what you have learned in class by identifying scenes from the video to illustrate your understanding. Similarly, A 1-5 *Dangerous Minds* shows examples of leadership styles, assigned and indigenous leadership, and the challenges involved in being a leader. Again, the key in doing this activity successfully is in being observant and being able to apply content from your readings to the rapidly moving action in the video.

The last six activities enable you to explore particular aspects of social work practice with groups from the initial work in the preaffiliation stage of group development (A 1-6 *Design Your Own Icebreaking Activity,* A 1-7 *Role-playing First Sessions*) to an examination of the elements involved in addressing power and control issues and developing group cohesion (A 1-8 *28 Days,* A 1-9 *Depicting the Intimacy Stage-Role plays,* A 1-13 *Team Chowder*). Three activities focus directly on the use of program activities in groups, first by having you observe ways activities support human growth and development in two different settings, rural Maine (A 1-10 *Greenfingers*) and a prison in England (A 1-11 *Mattering*). Using what you have learned in the classroom through observing and participating in experiential activities and what you have seen in the videos, the culminating activity on this topic is the demonstration project (A 1-12 *Selecting and Implementing Group Work Activities*). You and the members of your task group will combine your knowledge of group work practice, skill base, and imaginations to produce an activity that you will implement in the classroom.

Each of the activities here and in succeeding chapters includes suggestions for connecting the classroom activity with professional practice situations. The parallel process between classroom learning and practical application in the social work setting is central to social work education. Be sure to make use of the Practitioner's Notes to make the connections between what you are experiencing in the classroom activities with ways you can transfer your learning to your practice setting.

ACTIVITY 1-1: Hypothesis Development through Arch Building

IN THE CLASSROOM: This cooperative activity will help you to see how the process of observation is central to hypothesis development in practice. It will also highlight how the explicit and implicit assumptions we make affect theory building and the subsequent practice interventions evolving from that theory.

IN THE FIELD: Arch building requires well-developed eye-hand coordination, small muscle control, patience, and a willingness to cooperate with team members. For use in the practice situation, the activity may be contraindicated for children with low impulse control or with group members who are easily frustrated or discouraged. You can use *Arch Building* at various stages of group development. In the preaffiliation stage, you might use it to assess and encourage cooperative activity among group members in both task and treatment groups. It can also help you to assess members' physical skill levels (e.g., small muscle control, eye-hand coordination). When the group moves into power and control, you might introduce this activity to illustrate effective/ineffective communication. In the intimacy stage, you might use this activity to illustrate differences in observation and interpretation of behavior. In staff development groups, this activity can raise workers' awareness of the role that assumptions play in the hypotheses they develop in their work with client systems.

You can vary the conditions for building the arch to illustrate or influence the hypothesis development. Builder teams may be composed as homogeneous groups according to gender, age range, skill or other demographic variable, or as heterogeneous groups. Builder teams may be permitted to discuss the process as they build the arch or may be instructed to build the arch non-verbally.

MATERIALS: One set of catenary arch or Roman arch blocks*, level surface for building the arch (e.g., desk or table with chairs for the Builders); newsprint; thick markers; masking tape.

GROUP SIZE: 6-9 minimum

TIME REQUIRED: 30-40 minutes

SPACE REQUIREMENTS: A classroom with space for the Builder teams to construct the arch and for the Observer team(s) to see the activity without crowding the Builders. If the activity will involve more than one Builders team, a location where the remaining team(s) can wait their turn without seeing other teams as they make their attempt to build the arch is necessary.

PREPARATION: The instructor will be responsible for providing the arch kit and other supplies and for arranging the room with a center for arch building and space for observers to see the activity easily.

INSTRUCTIONS: Before the activity begins you should review the role of observation in hypothesis development based on readings and lecture/discussion content previously discussed in either your practice or research courses. Once the instructor has reviewed the goal of the activity with the class and has explained the procedures, you will have an opportunity to ask questions to clarify any areas that need further explanation. Decide whether you will volunteer to be on a Builder or Observer team. Builders teams consist of one or more groups with three members; Observers teams also will have three members per team.

Sequential Arch Building & Observation: If your class is using more than one team of Builders, the remaining Builders Team will leave the room. Observer team(s) will watch and make notes of significant data as members of the first Builders Team attempt to build the arch (5 minutes). When the first Builders Team has used their time, the next Builders Team, if any, will make their attempts. Observer teams complete an observation for subsequent Builder Teams' attempts to build the arch (5 minutes each). When all the Builders Teams have finished, the Observer Teams will move to separate locations to discuss their observations and work on their hypotheses. The Builders team(s) will meet separately also to discuss their experience and develop an hypothesis.

Hypothesis Development: Based on data observed, the team's value base and assumptions, each Observer team will develop an hypothesis about the process of arch building and post their hypothesis on the newsprint provided, writing in letters large enough so the hypothesis can be read across the room. Similarly, Builder teams will develop their hypotheses as participant observers (10 minutes).

Discussion: When the teams reconvene as a class, the groups will post their hypotheses so the entire class can read the newsprint. Using the questions below, the instructor will lead a discussion of the process and the outcome.

> On what is the hypothesis based?
>
> What are the assumptions?
>
> What values come into play?
>
> What might be the unintended consequences?

PRACTITIONER'S NOTES:

- With what types of groups would you use this activity?

- At what stage(s) of group development would this activity be useful?

- How would member's characteristics, skills, and abilities influence the way you would modify and implement this activity?

- How would this activity contribute to the group goals, members' goals, and session goals?

- At what point in the group meeting would you introduce the activity?

- How would you evaluate the usefulness and impact of the activity on the group and its members?

*Catenary arch kits are available from Summit Learning. ABS and Edmund Scientific supply Roman arch kits. See Catalog Resources for details.

Source: From an exercise created by Jane Peller, Associate Professor of Social Work, Northeastern Illinois University, Chicago. Adapted with permission.

ACTIVITY 1-2: The Ecosystems Machine

IN THE CLASSROOM: *The Ecosystems Machine* will reinforce the reading you have done on Ecosystems Theory. It will illustrate how human systems grow and change, show the interconnectedness of the elements of a system, and how a change in one part of the system affects the system as a whole.

IN THE FIELD: With a name change (e.g., The Teen Machine or The Group-Mobile, if allowing the resulting "machine" to move rather than stay in one spot), you can use this activity at the power and control or intimacy stages to help portray the interconnectedness and interdependence of the group members and to facilitate discussion on related topics. You can construct the machine using only sound and movement with no actual physical contact among participants. If the group is very large, you can ask for 10-15 volunteers to create the machine and have the remaining group members become observers. If the group is small enough and the members have enough large motor control, the machine may be allowed to move around the room as long as contact between the participants is maintained. Although the activity is highly interactive and physical, with suitable adaptation, it is workable for participants with most physical challenges. With any group where you plan to use this activity, you should consider the group members who will take part in the activity to determine what, if any, adaptations you should make to allow everyone to take part comfortably. Make the needed changes to the instructions.

If you are involved in in-service training, you could use *The Ecosystems Machine* as a lighthearted and engaging approach for introducing systems concepts in staff training, group supervision, and professional development workshops. In group supervision you might use this activity to facilitate discussion of ways to enhance teamwork.

MATERIALS: Readings on systems theory [e.g. Ecological Systems Theory in J.B. Ashford, C.W. LeCroy, & K.L. Lortie (2001). *Human behavior in the social environment (2nd ed.).* Belmont, CA: Brooks/Cole, pp. 105-108; Systems Theory in R.W. Toseland & R.F. Rivas (2001). *An introduction to group work practice (4th ed.).* Boston: Allyn & Bacon, pp.59-62.].

GROUP SIZE: 30-40

TIME REQUIRED: 20-30 minutes, depending on group size.

SPACE REQUIREMENTS: Large, open area plus seating for the debriefing at the end of the activity. If the activity takes place indoors, be sure to close doors and make an effort to keep the noise down to a level acceptable for the physical setting.

PREPARATION: Before the activity takes place, you should read and discuss the material on systems concepts. On the day of the activity, the instructor will be responsible for preparing the area by clearing a space in the meeting room to support the activity.

INSTRUCTIONS: This activity will offer you a way to have a visual, auditory, and kinesthetic experience of a fanciful human system that the class will begin to create. As the activity progresses, class members will add to the ecosystem machine's growth and development and then wind it down until it disappears.

Each of you will help to create the ecosystems machine by choosing a sound and movement that you can sustain without too much strain for a period of 5-10 minutes. While the activity is taking place, you should listen and observe the life of the machine closely in its various phases of operation, particularly when it is fully operational. Does it remain static? Are there subtle changes in each person's movement and sound as others join. What are the initial participants feeling as the machine grows and changes? How does the machine look and sound as participants leave one by one? How do participants feel in the winding down process? What happens to the machine and to those remaining as the others leave?

Creating the ecosystems machine: Decide when you will volunteer. You can help to begin the process by beginning phase of the machine. If you are part of the beginning phase, choose a spot in the open space and begin making a sound and an accompanying movement, such as moving an arm bent at the elbow back and forth and accentuating the movement by making a rhythmic sound (e.g., clanking, whooshing, or whistling). You might choose to be the second participant and join the first participant. You will choose a movement that somehow corresponds to the first person's movement and make a sound different from the first participant's sound to accompany the movement you have selected. The second participant should be touching the first participant at some point and should somehow correspond to, complement, or accentuate with the first participant's movement and sound. One by one, the remaining class members will join the machine, making the machine larger, louder, more complex, more integrated, more diverse, and more involved. When the machine has reached full size with all the class members playing a part in the machine's functioning, the machine will continue to operate for at least one minute.

Dismantling the machine: After the final minute has elapsed, you will choose when to leave the machine one by one and be seated. You should continue observing the machine as the winding down process evolves.

Discussion: When the machine is completely dismantled, the instructor will facilitate a discussion focusing on the observations you made during the activity. You should consider the nature of systems and the impact of change illustrated here by the adding and subtracting of participants. Connect your observations to the readings and the connections you see between systems concepts and elements of the activity.

PRACTITIONER'S NOTES:

- With what types of groups would you use this activity?

- At what stage(s) of group development would this activity be useful?

- How would member's characteristics, skills, and abilities influence the way you would modify and implement this activity?

- How would this activity contribute to the group goals, members' goals, and session goals?

- At what point in the group meeting would you introduce the activity?

- How would you evaluate the usefulness and impact of the activity on the group and its members?

Source: Contributed by Nancy A. Kelly, MSW, Field Coordinator, University of Maine School of Social Work. Used with permission.

ACTIVITY 1-3: Applying Theory in Practice

IN THE CLASSROOM: Participating in this activity will help you to gain some practice in applying your knowledge of social work theories to the practice skill of contracting.

IN THE FIELD: *Applying Theory in Practice* is suitable for you to use in on-going staff in-service training or in professional development workshops. You should have the group complete brief readings on the selected practice theories. You might also prepare and deliver mini-lectures and facilitate discussion before the group does the activity. You can vary the format by selecting different practice scenarios and emphasizing different practice theories that can vary the exercise format. For example, Johnson and Yanca (2001) list 21 possible practice theories, including the ones used in this activity. Depending on the time available, you can expand or limit the items the breakout you ask the groups to complete on the contract form. For example, other items might include tasks to be completed by the client and by the worker, the time limits of each aspect of the intervention, the intervention schedule, evaluation methods. However limited or expanded the number of items addressed in the contracting section, you should remind the participants that all items are important for effective contracting in the practice setting and that the ones selected are for illustrating the process in a limited way.

MATERIALS: Readings on theory (e.g., Johnson, L.C. & Yanca, S.J. (2001) *Social work practice: A generalist approach (7/e)*. Boston: Allyn & Bacon, Appendix, Models of Social Work Practice; Pillari, V. (2002). *Social work practice: Theory and skills*. Boston: Allyn & Bacon, Ch. 3 Knowledge.); readings on contracting (e.g., Kirst-Ashman, K.K. & Hull, G.H. (2002). *Understanding generalist practice (3ʳᵈ ed.)*, Pacific Grove, CA: Brooks/Cole, Ch. 6, Planning in Generalist Practice); instructions, theory summaries, contract forms, one per group.

GROUP SIZE: 30 maximum

TIME REQUIRED: 50 minutes (10 minutes for instructions and questions, 30 minutes for breakout groups to complete the exercise; 10 minutes for selected report from the breakout groups)

SPACE REQUIREMENTS: A meeting room to accommodate the whole group plus enough breakout spaces for each task group to complete the exercise with a minimum of interruption and background noise.

PREPARATION: Complete the assigned readings on the selected theories and on the use of contracting in social work practice.

INSTRUCTIONS: Before you begin the activity review the instructions, Theory Summaries and the contract form below. Ask any questions and/or raise points for clarification by the instructor. You should note that this contract form is abbreviated for purposes of this exercise and includes only two of the items usually contained in a typical written contract between client systems and worker(s).

You will join as small task group. The task groups will have 30 minutes to complete the exercise. Your instructor will be available for consultation if groups need it. About five minutes before the 30 minutes have elapsed, your group should begin to wrap up your work on your Contract Forms. When 30 minutes have elapsed, you will reconvene as a class. As time permits, two or three volunteer recorder/reporters will present their issues and goal statements. Offer your response to each presentation. Consider how well each group has used the theory to support their work on the contract elements. The instructor may wish to collect the Contract Forms for comments. If so, the instructor will return the forms in the next session.

PRACTITIONER'S NOTES:

- With what types of groups would you use this activity?

- At what stage(s) of group development would this activity be useful?

- How would member's characteristics, skills, and abilities influence the way you would modify and implement this activity?

- How would this activity contribute to the group goals, members' goals, and session goals?

- At what point in the group meeting would you introduce the activity?

- How would you evaluate the usefulness and impact of the activity on the group and its members?

APPLYING THEORY IN PRACTICE

Task Group Instructions

Select a recorder/reporter. Using one of the following situations, choose a theory from the five listed below. Using the theory to inform your practice, the group will act as consultants to the hypothetical worker. The group will collaborate to develop a contract for working on the issue with the client system. For today's session the group will focus on only two items for the contract: specifying the issue(s) and identifying the goal(s). The goal statements should include (a) what will be done, (b) under what conditions it will be done, and (c) what will be needed to attain the agreed-upon goal(s). Note briefly the way the theory supports the development of the goal statements.

Situations:

A.   Parents and teen are in conflict over curfew violations. The parents have sought help to resolve the situation at the local community center. They have been referred to a family mediation group offered at the center.

B.   Parent mandated to attend parent education group is habitually late to meetings. The worker will address the problem with the client at the next session.

C.   Community has experienced five accidents (one fatality) at a busy corner with no traffic light or stop sign. A group of residents have approached the neighborhood settlement house staff for help in dealing with the city.

D.   Counseling center group worker convenes voluntary group of college students wanting to manage severe test anxiety.

E.   Task group elected to program planning committee at Bangor Senior Center meets with the program director to plan events for next month.

SUMMARIES OF SELECTED THEORIES

1. <u>Life Model</u>: Assessment carried out by worker and client together seeking tounderstand meaning; focus on person and problem to set objectives and design appropriate action. Engages positive forces in client and environment. Attempts to remove environmental obstacles and change negative transactions.... Action designed to increase self-esteem, problem solving, and coping skills. Also works to facilitate group functioning and influence organizational structure, social networks, and physical settings.

2. <u>Locality Development</u>: Assessment is problem solving with citizens.... The goal is the development of community capacity and integration.... Citizens participate in interactional problem solving. Involves a broad cross-section of people. Uses small task-oriented groups that seek consensus. Problem solving is primary.

3. <u>Mediating Group Model</u>: Assessment is a systems assessment of the blocks to need fulfillment. Focus is on individual in interaction, group process, and impinging environment.... Goals related to mutual need for self-fulfillment as individual and society reach out to each other. Clarifies communication and makes use of problem-solving process.

4. <u>Psychosocial Model</u>: Assessment is differential psychosocial diagnosis. Concerned with personality, etiology, and psychiatric classifications of disorders. Diagnosis very important. Goal is adjustment of the individual through change in perception, response, and communication. Relationship is prime concern. Uses reflection, interpretation, ventilation, support, and environmental manipulation.

5. <u>Sociobehavioral Model</u>: Assessment specifies behaviors, defines baselines, specifies stimulus, antecedents, and consequences. Frequency, magnitude, and direction of problem behavior are monitored during and following intervention. Goals are very specific to behavioral change.

Source: From Louise C. Johnson and Stephen J. Yanca, *Social work practice: A generalist approach, 7/e,* Published by Allyn & Bacon, Boston, MA. Copyright © 2001 by Pearson Education. Reprinted by permission of the publisher.

USING THEORY IN PRACTICE

Contract Form

Task Group Members:

> *Instructions:* Complete items 1 & 2. On a separate sheet, note the way the selected theory supports the statement of the problem(s)/issue(s) and the development of the goal statements. The forms will be collected during the report to the larger group and returned at the next session with comments.

1. problem(s)/issue(s) [limit 3]

    a.

    b.

    c.

2. specific goals for each problem

    a.

    b.

    c.

ACTIVITY 1-4: Illustrating Stages of Group Development - *The Breakfast Club* [Rated R]

IN THE CLASSROOM: Viewing *The Breakfast Club* will help you to gain skill in observing and identifying stages of group development as depicted in the video. Discussion of what you observed in the video will help to reinforce content on the stages of group development from assigned readings.

IN THE FIELD: You might use this activity in staff training to introduce and explore the stages of group development as a useful way of assessing groups in the practice setting. Selected readings on group dynamics and the stages of group development from basic texts should precede the use of the video (see "Materials"). You might also use *The Breakfast Club* with teen groups as an entertaining and non-threatening way to raise issues of interpersonal relations among teens and between teens and adults, roles teens assume or have thrust upon them, and/or the phenomenon and impact of cliques on teens. You would adapt the instruction sheet with questions appropriate to the discussion topic as a tool for the teens to use to record their observations, reactions, and comments. If you eliminate the instruction sheet, be sure to prepare several questions to stimulate group discussion. For groups where some members have hearing loss, use a video with subtitles.

You may substitute other formulations of the stages of group development for the Garland, Jones, and Kolodny (1973) five-stage model—preaffiliation, power and control, intimacy, differentiation, separation (e.g., Tuckman's (1963) rhyming stages—forming, storming, norming, performing or Henry's (1992) five stages—initiating, convening, conflict, maintenance, termination). You can increase the complexity of the exercise by asking group members to compare and contrast two or more models, evaluating the applicability and utility of each model in analyzing the dynamics of the group shown in the video. To include a discussion of the ways gender may affect the group's progression through the stages, you can read Shiller's (1997) feminist formulation, "preaffiliation, establishing a relational base, mutuality and interpersonal empathy, challenge and change, termination."

When you use videos, you should always do a preview and take notes on the points you want to emphasize with the group. Then you could create a viewing guide similar to the one you will use in this activity. You will need expanded space for group members to take adequate notes. You will also need to adapt the instructions to the group situation where it will be used and duplicate enough copies of the viewing guide for group members. In addition to the viewing guide, you will also prepare discussion questions. If time does not permit showing the video and holding the discussion in the same session, view the video in one session. Ask group members to make quick notes on the viewing guide and expand the notes between sessions in preparation for the later discussion.

MATERIALS: Readings on stages of group development [e.g., Anderson, J. (1997). *Social work with groups: A process model.* New York: Longman, pp. 99-106; Toseland, R.W. & Rivas, R.F. (2001). *An introduction to group work practice (4ᵗʰ ed.).* Boston: Allyn & Bacon, pp. 88-93. See additional suggested readings below.]; video of *The Breakfast Club*; VCR and television available to students for viewing the video before the session for those who do not have access to a VCR at home; Viewing Guides for taking notes during the viewing.

GROUP SIZE: 30-50

TIME REQUIRED: One hour and 32 minutes viewing time before the session; 25 minutes of class time—15 minutes task group discussion, 10 minutes for group reports to the class.

SPACE REQUIREMENTS: Classroom with sufficient seating for students to engage in discussion as a group plus breakout spaces for small group discussion.

PREPARATION: Complete the assigned readings on aspects of group development. Review the Viewing Guide with directions for taking notes during the video and raise any questions you might have. You may want to watch the video in small groups outside class time. Sharing the rental with a small group of class members will reduce costs.

INSTRUCTIONS: *For viewing the video:* Using the Viewing Guide below, view the video and make your notes independently. Bring the notes to class to facilitate your participation in the group discussion.

For the group discussion: Divide into task groups of five to seven students per group. In your task group, compare notes on your analyses of the video and develop a composite report to share with the whole group during the report to the class. As part of the discussion, you should also compare and contrast your observations from the video with your own experiences with groups either as members or as group workers and be ready to contribute those findings to the discussion.

PRACTITIONER'S NOTES:

- With what types of groups would you use this activity?

- At what stage(s) of group development would this activity be useful?

- How would member's characteristics, skills, and abilities influence the way you would modify and implement this activity?

- How would this activity contribute to the group goals, members' goals, and session goals?

- At what point in the group meeting would you introduce the activity?

- How would you evaluate the usefulness and impact of the activity on the group and its members?

ANALYSIS OF *The Breakfast Club*

Instructions: Rent a copy of *The Breakfast Club* from a local video rental store. View the video a day or two before the session where we will discuss the video as an illustration of the stages of group development according to Garland, Jones, and Kolodny (1973). Use the directions below to guide your note taking while you view the video.

1. Before you view the video, complete the assigned readings on stages of group development. Using the space below, name and define each phase of group development according to Garland, Jones, and Kolodny (1973).

2. Choose a situation from the film, which clearly illustrates each phase, giving enough detail to recall the situation for later discussion.

3. State your reasons for choosing each example.

Additional suggested readings:

Garland, J.A., Jones, H.E., and Kolodny, R.L. (1973). A model for stages of development in social work groups (17-71). In S. Bernstein. *Explorations in group work: Essays in theory and practice.* Boston, MA: Milford House Inc.

Henry, S. (1992). *Group skills in social work: A four-dimensional approach (2nd ed.).* Pacific Grove, CA: Brooks/Cole Publishing Co., 21.

Schiller, L.Y. (1997). Rethinking stages of development in women's groups: Implications for practice. *Social Work with Groups, 20*(3), 4.

Tuckman, B. (1963). Developmental sequence in small groups. *Psychological Bulletin, 63,* 384-399.

ACTIVITY 1-5: Illustrating Group Leadership - *Dangerous Minds* [Rated R]

IN THE CLASSROOM: *Dangerous Minds* illustrates content on the group leadership from your assigned reading. Viewing this video will help you to gain skill in observing and identifying designated and indigenous leaders, leadership styles and skills, and leading groups in a cross-cultural setting as depicted in the video. This video will also raise issues for you about social work practice in a host setting.

IN THE FIELD: *Dangerous Minds* may be used as part of an in-service training or professional development workshop particularly with practitioners working with groups of adolescents. You can also use this video directly with teen groups as a discussion starter for a range of topics: school issues, dealing with authority, gangs, violence, prejudice and discrimination. For groups where members have hearing loss, you may be able to obtain a video with subtitles. *One Flew Over the Cuckoos Nest* is another video illustrating indigenous leadership and the uses of authority in an in-patient setting [Rated R, playing time – two hours, 14 minutes]. You might substitute this video if you cannot find *Dangerous Minds*.

MATERIALS: Readings on group leadership; leadership and diversity [e.g., Toseland, R.W. & Rivas, R.F. (2001) *An introduction to group work practice (4ᵗʰ ed.)*. Boston: Allyn & Bacon, Ch. 4]; Viewing Guides; VCR, TV, videotape of *Dangerous Minds*.

GROUP SIZE: 30-40

TIME REQUIRED: Viewing time outside class – 99 minutes; discussion time – 20-40 minutes, depending on class size and discussion format chosen.

SPACE REQUIREMENTS: Classroom with sufficient seating for class members to engage in discussion as a group plus breakout spaces for small group discussion.

PREPARATION: Complete the assigned readings. Review the Viewing Guide and raise any points for clarification. If you plan to view the video with a small group of class members to reduce costs, make plans well before the session where the class will discuss group leadership. In either case, view the video one or two days before the scheduled class discussion.

INSTRUCTIONS: Divide into task groups of five to seven students per group. In your small group, compare notes on your analyses of the video and develop a composite report to share with the whole group during a report-back period. Also, compare and contrast the observations from the video with your own experiences with groups either as members or as group workers and be ready to contribute those findings to the discussion.

PRACTITIONER'S NOTES:

- With what types of groups would you use this activity?

- At what stage(s) of group development would this activity be useful?

- How would member's characteristics, skills, and abilities influence the way you would modify and implement this activity?

- How would this activity contribute to the group goals, members' goals, and session goals?

- At what point in the group meeting would you introduce the activity?

- How would you evaluate the usefulness and impact of the activity on the group and its members?

INSTRUCTIONS AND VIEWING GUIDE - *Dangerous Minds*

Instructions: View the video using the Viewing Guide below. Identify and record scenes in the video that illustrate group leadership styles and skills. Note implications for social work practice in working with teens in a host setting. Be prepared to discuss the video in the next session, applying content from the readings to relevant scenes from the video.

Viewing Guide: Identify scenes from the video that illustrate the following:

- Designated leaders' styles:

- Indigenous leaders' styles:

- Facilitation skills:

- Cross-cultural issues:

- Uses of power:

- Managing conflict:

- Other pertinent observations:

ACTIVITY 1-6: Design Your Own Icebreaking Activity

IN THE CLASSROOM: As you work together with your task group, you will learn how to develop an ice-breaking activity based on your own experiences, creativity, and imagination.

IN THE FIELD: You can use this activity with program planning groups and "train the trainer" workshops. At points where a group has vetoed the previously planned activity, this activity can be adapted and used in a variety of situations beyond the icebreaker if the worker keeps an "emergency kit" of bags and props. Items in the kits should be safe for the age and skill level of group members. You can also instruct the group to divide into teams and design activities without benefit of props if you outline the instructions clearly. This activity can be used with other stages of group development as the focal point. For example, in the separation stage props recalling events in the life of the group may be used to develop skits summing up the group experience.

MATERIALS: The instructor will be responsible for supplying previously prepared lunch bags containing props for the creation of the activity. Possible props include small puppets, markers, tape, construction paper, beanbag or "koosh" ball, pencils and paper, or a "prop-less" bag with instructions to create a verbal activity. As a variation, the instructor may ask the class to supply the props and make up the prop bags at the beginning of the activity.

GROUP SIZE: 10-20

TIME REQUIRED: 30-45 minutes

SPACE REQUIREMENTS: An area with sufficient space for the class to divide into teams, create, and demonstrate the activity.

PREPARATION: If the instructor has asked the class to supply the props, you should gather items well before the class session and remember to bring them to class on the day of the activity.

INSTRUCTIONS: Divide into small teams of three to four students, select a prop bag, and choose a location to work on your activity design. You will have 15 minutes to create the activity using the props in the bag. When the class reconvenes, volunteer to describe or demonstrate your activity. At the end of each demonstration the class will provide feedback to each group on what worked well and what might be done differently. As you observe each other's activities, consider what adaptation might be needed for diverse groups and for individual members with limitations.

PRACTITIONER'S NOTES:

- With what types of groups would you use this activity?

- At what stage(s) of group development would this activity be useful?

- How would member's characteristics, skills, and abilities influence the way you would modify and implement this activity?

- How would this activity contribute to the group goals, members' goals, and session goals?

- At what point in the group meeting would you introduce the activity?

- How would you evaluate the usefulness and impact of the activity on the group and its members?

ACTIVITY 1-7: Role-playing First Sessions

IN THE CLASSROOM: This activity will help you to think about the themes present in the preaffiliation stage of group development, particularly in the first session with the group and to begin to develop approaches to dealing with those themes effectively.

IN THE FIELD: You might select this activity for use with groups where members are reluctant to participate in the group. A scripted skit rather than a role-play gives some structure and safety to group members' participation and might be useful in initiating discussion of the issues that have convened the group [e.g., a group of teens who are making the transition from the foster care system to emancipation]. You can also use this activity in staff in-service training or in a professional development workshop focusing on enhancing skills in practice with groups. In developing the role-play scenarios or in scripting the skits, you must take care to raise those issues with which the group is willing and able to deal in this preliminary stage of development.

MATERIALS: Readings on issues in first sessions [e.g., Shulman, L. (1999). *The skills of helping individuals, families, groups, and communities (4th ed.).* Itasca, IL: F.E. Peacock Publishers, Inc., Chs. 9 & 10].

GROUP SIZE: 30

TIME REQUIRED: 50 minutes minimum.

SPACE REQUIREMENTS: Classroom space sufficient for the class to engage in the activity.

PREPARATION: Complete the assigned readings and reflect on the issues involved in first sessions. Also consider your own experience in first sessions in classes or other groups.

INSTRUCTIONS: Read the instruction sheet and raise points needing clarification. As a class, choose one of the situations listed on the instruction sheet. The instructor will ask for six to eight volunteers to play group members and a volunteer to play the group worker. The group and identified worker will role-play the first 5-10 minutes of the first session incorporating issues identified by the practice text [e.g., "tuning in" to concerns (Shulman, 1999, pp. 45-48)]. If you have not volunteered to be in the role-play, follow the instructions for Observers. During the discussion, share your observations and link your observations to the readings.

PRACTITIONER'S NOTES:

- With what types of groups would you use this activity?

- At what stage(s) of group development would this activity be useful?

- How would member's characteristics, skills, and abilities influence the way you would modify and implement this activity?

- How would this activity contribute to the group goals, members' goals, and session goals?

- At what point in the group meeting would you introduce the activity?

- How would you evaluate the usefulness and impact of the activity on the group and its members?

ROLE-PLAY: *Facilitating the First Group Session*

PURPOSE: To practice skills needed in the first stage of group development in a simulated first session.

INSTRUCTIONS TO THE GROUP: Select one scenario from those listed below for the selected players to role-play.

Sample scenarios:

> *parent education group - worker who is single, has no kids
> *transition to community living-adolescents in foster care group - worker (age 53)
> *teen parents support group - male worker
> *school-age boys activity group living in an in-patient psychiatric setting - worker in early 20s
> *African-American community action group - non-African-American worker
> *AIDS awareness young adult group - female/male co-workers

INSTRUCTIONS TO THE PLAYERS: In the allotted 10 minutes preparation time, choose someone to play the group worker. Discuss what roles the remaining players will take as group members. Briefly discuss how your role-play will illustrate the issues identified in the readings as important to consider in beginning the work with the group in the first session.

Present the role-play [5-10 minutes]. Resume your own identities and participate in debriefing discussion led by the instructor.

INSTRUCTIONS TO THE OBSERVERS: Using the information in the readings to guide your notes, observe the role-play. When the role-play is concluded, participate in the debriefing discussion led by the instructor.

OBSERVER'S NOTES:

ACTIVITY 1-8: Illustrating Group Cohesion -
28 Days [Rated PG-13]

IN THE CLASSROOM: *28 Days* illustrates content on group cohesion from the assigned
readings. It shows the development of group cohesion through planned activities and
contacts among group members in the milieu of the in-patient, substance abuse treatment
setting. Viewing this video will help you to gain skill in identifying how group cohesion
develops.

IN THE FIELD: You can use this activity in staff in-service training sessions and professional
development workshops where participants have done some preliminary study of group
dynamics. Duplicating short reading assignments for workshop participants and asking
them to read the material a few days before you show the video generally works well. You
might also use it with groups in the practice setting as a discussion starter to raise issues
pertinent to group dynamics in a non-threatening way. For groups where members have
hearing loss, a video with closed-captioning may permit use of the activity.

MATERIALS: Readings on group dynamics [e.g., Toseland, R.W. & Rivas, R.F. (2001). *An
introduction to group work practice (4th ed.).* Boston: Allyn & Bacon, Ch. 3.]; Viewing Guides,
VCR, TV, videotape of *28 Days.*

GROUP SIZE: 30-40

TIME REQUIRED: Viewing time outside class – 104 minutes; 30 minutes class time—20
minutes for task group discussion, 10 minutes for group reports and class discussion.

SPACE REQUIREMENTS: Classroom with sufficient seating for group discussion.

PREPARATION: In the session before the discussion, review the Viewing Guide for the analysis
of the video. Raise points needing clarification. If you plan to view the video with a small
group of class members to reduce costs, make those arrangements well in advance of the
session where the class will discuss group cohesion. View the video using the Viewing
Guide.

INSTRUCTIONS: Divide into task groups of five to seven students. Select a reporter. Compare
your Viewing Guide notes on your analyses of the video, and develop a composite report
to share with the class during the report-back period. Also compare/contrast observations
from the video with your own experiences with groups either as a member or a group
worker. Link your observations to content from the readings. Contribute your findings to
the discussion.

As a group, summarize your findings. When the 20 minutes have elapsed, reconvene as a
class for the group reports. The instructor will facilitate a discussion of the findings.

PRACTITIONER'S NOTES:

- With what types of groups would you use this activity?

- At what stage(s) of group development would this activity be useful?

- How would member's characteristics, skills, and abilities influence the way you would modify and implement this activity?

- How would this activity contribute to the group goals, members' goals, and session goals?

- At what point in the group meeting would you introduce the activity?

- How would you evaluate the usefulness and impact of the activity on the group and its members?

INSTRUCTIONS AND VIEWING GUIDE - 28 Days

Instructions: View the video using the Viewing Guide below. Identify and record scenes in the video that illustrate aspects of group dynamics, particularly group cohesion, as demonstrated by the interactions between the patients at the rehabilitation facility. Note implications for social work practice in working with adults in an in-patient setting. Be prepared to discuss the video in the next session, applying content from the readings to relevant scenes from the video.

Viewing Guide: Identify scenes from the video that illustrate the following:

- Group roles supporting or undermining group cohesion:

- Indigenous leadership supporting or undermining group cohesion:

- Communication patterns:

- Facilitation skills supporting or undermining group cohesion:

- Instances of social control:

- Indicators of group cohesion:

- Implications for practice:

- Other pertinent observations:

ACTIVITY 1-9: Depicting the Intimacy Stage – Role-plays

IN THE CLASSROOM: This activity will illustrate issues in the intimacy stage of group development as they intersect with age and gender. It will offer you opportunities for hands-on experience in creating an activity to enhance group cohesion in a simulated group, provide a way to sharpen your observational skills, and learn how to provide a constructive critique.

IN THE FIELD: Role-plays illustrating aspects of group development or focusing on group facilitation skills are well suited to professional development workshops and staff in-service training events. Time is the major consideration in using this activity. If your group is large, spreading the presentations over several sessions gives each task group ample time to make their presentations and hold a full follow-up discussion.

MATERIALS: Role-play instruction sheets; chairs for the teen and women's groups; toys and other props for the toddlers' group; video camera and tapes to record the role-plays [optional].

GROUP SIZE: 30

TIME REQUIRED: 25 minutes per role-play—10 minutes for the role-play; 5 minutes for Observer Task Groups to prepare critique; 10 minutes for the discussion. Depending on the length of individual group session, role-plays may be extended over several sessions to insure that each group has ample time for presentation and discussion.

SPACE REQUIREMENTS: Classroom with enough space for the observers to view the role-play and for the camera to record the action, plus a cleared space where the role-plays can be performed.

PREPARATION: *One session before the activity*—Read the role-play scenarios given below. Form task groups. Your task group will select one scenario to present to the whole group at the next session. When all the scenarios have been selected, adjourn to your task group's breakout area to prepare for your role-play presentations. In your task group meeting, the group will distribute the roles among members and discuss what props role-players will bring to enhance their roles as group members or as the worker. Your group will collaborate with the worker in developing the activity to enhance group cohesion. Your group will also select a member who will facilitate the discussion with the class following the role-play. Your task group will devise questions that the facilitator will use with the class to ask for feedback in critiquing the application of group work skills and principles in the role-play. If time permits, you may practice the role-play in preparation for presentation at the next session or schedule a time to meet before the next session to do the needed preparation.

During the role-plays and discussion—In addition to presenting one role-play, each task group will observe the role-plays of the other groups and take notes on the use of group work skills and principles. You will participate in the discussions led by the facilitator from each of the other role-play groups.

PRACTITIONER'S NOTES:
- With what types of groups would you use this activity?

- At what stage(s) of group development would this activity be useful?

- How would member's characteristics, skills, and abilities influence the way you would modify and implement this activity?

- How would this activity contribute to the group goals, members' goals, and session goals?

- At what point in the group meeting would you introduce the activity?

- How would you evaluate the usefulness and impact of the activity on the group and its members?

ROLE PLAYS DEPICTING THE INTIMACY STAGE OF GROUP DEVELOPMENT

Instructions to the Task Groups

To the Role-Play Task Groups: Read the Role-play scenarios. Select one scenario to present to the whole group. Distribute the roles among task group members. Discuss what props Players will bring to enhance their roles as group members or as the worker. Collaborate with the designated worker to develop an activity to enhance group cohesion. Decide who will facilitate the discussion following the role-play. Practice the role-play in preparation for presentation at the next session. Decide what questions the facilitator will use to ask for feedback in critiquing the application of group work skills and principles. On the day of the role-play, bring the props. Arrange the furniture in the meeting room to support the role-play. Conduct the role-play. Allow the Observers to meet for five minutes to prepare their comments. Reconvene the group, and facilitate the discussion.

To the Observer Task Groups: Observe the role-plays. Make notes on the use of group work skills and principles. Participate in the discussion facilitated by a member of the Players group.

Time Limits: 10 minutes per group for the role-play; 5 minutes for Observer Task Groups to prepare critique; 10 minutes for the discussion.

TEEN MOMS GROUP

The Teen Moms Group has been meeting weekly at a local church under the auspices of the Adolescent Parenting Intervention Project. The Project provides support and secondary prevention services to teens who are pregnant or parenting. The Teen Moms Group provides support and parenting education services through group discussion, guest speakers, and recreational services. These five young women have been meeting with the worker for ten weeks. The program operates on a year-round basis.

Soledad: Soledad (15) lives at home with her mother and two younger sisters, ages 11 and 13. She no longer sees the father of her twins. Her mother won't allow it. She is very outspoken about the unfairness of her mother's attitude. Soledad has lots of experience taking care of her younger sisters and doesn't think she needs this group. She tends to dominate the group discussion by focusing on her individual problems.

Cristina: Cristina (16) is living with her boyfriend and his family. She is pregnant again. She is somewhat withdrawn and seems very unhappy about the way she is treated by her boyfriend's family. Because she is not in school or working, they expect her to do most of the housework and cooking. She is responsible for childcare during the day, but when her boyfriend's mother gets home from work, she takes over the parenting role with the toddler. This week the teen mom has some bruises on her arms that she has tried to cover with makeup.

Sheila: Sheila (17) and her two children have their own apartment in public housing. Her son, age 3 _, attends a local Headstart program. She flaunts her competence in living on her own. She attempts to tell the others how they should handle any problem that they raise for discussion.

Robin: Robin (17) lives with her parents who care for her child while she works at Wendy's. She is very quiet and doesn't participate much.

Lisa: Lisa (14) lives in a foster family with her infant daughter. She is attending a new school sporadically and having some difficulty adjusting to being back in the classroom. She talks about dropping out, becoming emancipated, and having her own apartment. She admires Sheila and envies her situation.

TODDLERS GROUP

The Toddlers Group is a weekly recreational group that meets at the Family Services Center. All the children in this group are from Latino backgrounds. The goal of the group is to provide early intervention services for children who are considered at risk for developmental delays. This group has been together for three months. Only one of the children has been in a group before attending this program.

Tomas: This 2 1/2-year-old boy is very active and eager to join in an activity the group worker suggests.

Luz: This three-year-old twin girl is very feminine, likes only the "girl's" toys and dislikes any activity where she might get dirty.

Mirtia: This three-year-old twin girl is energetic and likes athletic challenges like bouncing on the trampoline.

Marcelo: This three-year-old boy is shy and needs to be coaxed to try every activity.

Roberto: This three-year-old boy is practically non-verbal in either English or Spanish. He likes to play quietly by himself, but is quite aggressive when other children try to join in the activity he has chosen.

THE TIGERS – A BOYS AFTER-SCHOOL GROUP

The Tigers, an after-school group of fourth graders, meet every day at the community center located in the center of the public housing complex where they live. They walk to the center together as a group with their after-school worker who picks them up in the schoolyard. The group has been together since mid-September. It is now early November. The after-school program provides a snack, an area to do homework, and space for organized games and other activities. It also has a secluded spot for reading and relaxing.

Joey: An only child who likes woodcrafts and anything he can make using tools. He reads only to figure out instructions. School is not his favorite place.

Tom: An athlete who loves active, competitive sports. He is well coordinated, always the leader in games, well liked and admired by the other boys.

Jeff: A studious child who favors the homework corner and the computer. He is the oldest of five children in his family and is conscientious about looking after his siblings. He transfers some of this behavior in his interactions with members of the after-school group.

Teddy: The youngest and smallest child in the group. He has asthma and regularly uses an inhaler. He likes crafts and table games. Occasionally he works on his homework or reads in the homework corner. He is first to the computers and is a very skilled on the Web.

Robert: The biggest and physically strongest child in the group. He likes aggressive games and sports. He is highly competitive on and off the playing field.

WOMEN'S SUPPORT GROUP

The Women's Support Group is sponsored by the YWCA Family Services Project. The current group has been meeting for 12 weeks and is staffed by a social worker and a field intern from the University's School of Social Work.

Alice Johnson (34) is married and has two grade-school children. She works part-time at the community center in the day care program as an aide. One of her children is developmentally disabled. Her husband was recently put on a 4-day workweek by the factory where he has been employed for the last 15 years.

Martha Pierce (33) also is married and has two grade-schoolers. The elder, a boy, was recently diagnosed as having a learning disability, but the school is resisting adding the necessary supports for instruction. Martha works part-time at a local factory. Martha's husband wants her to quit and take care of the children full time. He appears to blame her for their son's school difficulties.

Jennifer Miller (30) is a trust officer at a neighborhood bank. She recently purchased a condo and is considering becoming a foster parent for a school-age child. Her family is dismayed that she remains unmarried and frequently tries to find suitable dates for her.

Laura James (44) was recently divorced and is having problems with her adolescent children who perceive her as having driven their father away. She has just lost her job at Sears as a buyer for women's wear. Her husband is frequently late with his child support payments.

Sandra Greene (42) has been divorced for three years. She is a teacher at a local day care center. Her adolescent children are agitating to live with their father, although he is less enthusiastic about this plan than they are. Sandra feels betrayed.

ACTIVITY 1-10: Illustrating the Use of Horticulture as a Group Activity - *Greenfingers* [Rated R]

IN THE CLASSROOM: *Greenfingers* illustrates the use of horticulture as an intervention. Viewing this video will give you an opportunity to apply content on use of program activities from assigned readings.

IN THE FIELD: You can use this video as part of staff in-service training sessions and professional development workshops where participants have done some reading on the use of activities with groups. Duplicating short reading assignments for workshop participants and asking them to read the material a few days before you show the video generally works well. The video illustrates the development of group cohesion through unplanned and planned horticultural activities. For groups where members have hearing loss, a video with closed-captioning may permit use of the activity.

MATERIALS: Readings on activities [e.g., Whittaker, J.K. (1985). Program activities: Their selection and use in a therapeutic milieu. In M. Sundel et al. *Individual change through small groups (2nd ed.)*, pp. 237-250. New York: The Free Press. See additional suggested readings below.] Video of *Greenfingers*; VCR and television for viewing the video before the session; Viewing Guides for taking notes during the viewing, one per student.

GROUP SIZE: 30-50

TIME REQUIRED: Viewing time before the session–91 minutes; Class time–15 minutes discussion in task groups; 10 minutes for group reports and class discussion.

SPACE REQUIREMENTS: Classroom plus breakout spaces for small group discussion.

PREPARATION: Review the directions in the Viewing Guide below. Raise questions and/or points for clarification with your instructor. If you plan to view the video with a small group of class members to reduce costs, make those arrangements well in advance of the session where the class will discuss group cohesion. View the video and complete the observations required on the Viewing Guide.

INSTRUCTIONS: *For the group discussion -* Divide into task groups of five to seven students per group. Select a reporter who will give the group's findings during the class discussion. In your task group compare your Viewing Guide notes on your analyses of the video with those of other group members, and develop a composite report to share with the class during the report-back period. Also compare and contrast the observations from the video with your own experiences with groups either as members or as group workers. Share that information with the group. Link your observations to content from the readings on group cohesion. Be ready to contribute those findings to the discussion.

PRACTITIONER'S NOTES:

- With what types of groups would you use this activity?

- At what stage(s) of group development would this activity be useful?

- How would member's characteristics, skills, and abilities influence the way you would modify and implement this activity?

- How would this activity contribute to the group goals, members' goals, and session goals?

- At what point in the group meeting would you introduce the activity?

- How would you evaluate the usefulness and impact of the activity on the group and its members?

Additional Suggested Readings: Brandler, S. & Roman, C.P. (1991). *Group work skills and strategies for effective interventions.* (pp. 128-131). Binghamton, NY: Haworth Press.

Hewson, M. (1994). *Horticulture as therapy.* Guelph, Ontario: Greenmor Printing Company Limited.

Middleman, R.R. (1968). A guide to the analysis of non-verbal content. In R.R.

Middleman. *The non-verbal method in working with groups* (pp. 130-173). New York: Association Press.

Relf, P.D. (1990). The use of horticulture in vocational rehabilitation. *Journal of Rehabilitation, 47*(3), 53-56.

Vinter, R.D. (1985). Program activities: An analysis of their effects on participant behavior. In M. Sundel, P. Glasser, R. Sarri, and R. Vinter. *Individual change through small groups (2nd ed.)* (pp. 226-236). New York: The Free Press.

INSTRUCTIONS AND VIEWING GUIDE - Greenfingers

Instructions: View the video using the Viewing Guide below. Identify and record scenes in the video that illustrate aspects of group dynamics, particularly group cohesion, as demonstrated by the interactions between the patients at the rehabilitation facility. Note implications for social work practice in working with adults in an involuntary setting. Be prepared to discuss the video in the next session, applying content from the readings to relevant scenes from the video.

Viewing Guide: Identify scenes from the video that illustrate the following:

- Informal and formal uses of horticulture as an activity:

- Indigenous leadership in developing the horticultural program:

- Uses of authority in developing the horticultural program:

- Group roles:

- Indicators of group cohesion:

- Illustrations of the stages of group development:

- Implications for practice:

- Effects of the horticultural activities on the group members; within the institution; in the larger community:

- Other pertinent observations:

ACTIVITY 1-11: Illustrating the Match between the Group and the Activity - *Mattering*

IN THE CLASSROOM: In this video you will see the way program activities can be used with adolescents in a rural setting in Maine. Viewing the video will help you make connections with points from the readings suggested below.

IN THE FIELD: *Mattering* is useful as a training tool with peer group leaders and agency staff and for professional development workshops. If you don't have enough time to show the entire video, you could select clips to use as discussion starters. You might also use the video as a discussion starter with teens facing issues similar to those experienced by the teens in *Mattering*. Note that in some scenes the teens and the worker use language some may find offensive.

MATERIALS: Readings on selection and use of program activities [e.g., Preparing for group meetings. In R.W. Toseland, & R.F. Rivas. (2001). *An introduction to group work practice (4th ed.).* pp. 256-260, Boston: Allyn & Bacon; Whittaker, J.K. (1985). Program activities: Their selection and use in a therapeutic milieu. In M. Sundel, et al. *Individual change through small groups (2nd ed.)* pp. 237-250. New York: The Free Press.]; VCR, TV, videotape, viewing guide.

GROUP SIZE: 30-40

TIME REQUIRED: Viewing time – 57 minutes; discussion time – 20 minutes.

SPACE REQUIREMENTS: Seating space to view the video comfortably; space to form a circle for discussion.

PREPARATION: The instructor will arrange the room to support the activity, making sure that the seating configuration allows students to have an unobstructed view of the TV. The instructor will also check the equipment—the VCR, TV, volume of the soundtrack and make any needed adjustments before the session begins.

INSTRUCTIONS: Review the viewing guide to make sure you understand the instructions. Ask the instructor for clarification on any points that may be unclear. When the video starts, use the viewing guide below to take notes on the use of program activities at various stages of group development. Following the video, you will participate in a class discussion, giving your observations on the activities used in the video and making connections to the relevant points in the readings. Consider how the material in the readings and the video link with your experiences with using activities in groups in their field placement or with other groups you may have facilitated. Help to develop suggested standards for selecting and implementing activities that would be useful in the groups with whom you work.

PRACTITIONER'S NOTES:

- At what stage(s) of group development would this activity be useful?

- How would member's characteristics, skills, and abilities influence the way you would modify and implement this activity?

- How would this activity contribute to the group goals, members' goals, and session goals?

- At what point in the group meeting would you introduce the activity?

- How would you evaluate the usefulness and impact of the activity on the group and its members?

VIEWING GUIDE - Mattering

Instructions: As the video proceeds, note comments, questions, and reactions on the various points listed below. Bring the annotated viewing guide to the discussion.

1. Using the grid below, make brief notes to aid your recall for the discussion that will be held following the video. Record the activities shown in the video. Identify the stage of group development where the activity was implemented. Evaluate the appropriateness of the activity in relation to the stage of group development, the program and session goals, and the characteristics of the group members. Note any further observations or questions in the *Comments/Questions* column.

Activities Selected - Stage of Grp. Dev. - Appropriateness - Effectiveness - Comments/Questions

2. Comment on the worker's strategies in implementing activities with the group.

3. Note roles played by group members in the various activities.

ACTIVITY 1-12: Selecting and Implementing Group Work Activities - A Demonstration

IN THE CLASSROOM: In this activity you will apply group work principles in selecting and implementing program activities in a simulated practice situation.

IN THE FIELD: You can use this activity in a demonstration format in workshops for professional development and staff in-service training. You may also use this exercise for training agency volunteers and peer group leaders. Duplicating short reading assignments for workshop participants and asking them to read the material a few days before you show the video generally works well to provide them with a foundation for viewing the video and participating in the group discussion. To vary the activity to suit different group purposes and goals, you can substitute scenarios for different age groups and different settings or offer a range of scenarios to broaden the later discussion. Each task group could develop their own scenario if you present the instructions in the session before the activity will take place.

MATERIALS: Assigned readings [e.g., Whittaker, J.K. (1985). Program activities: Their selection and use in a therapeutic milieu. In M. Sundel et al. *Individual change through small groups* (2nd ed.), pp. 237-250. New York: The Free Press. See additional suggested readings below.]; assorted activity resource materials: crafts materials, table games, indoor toys [e.g., "koosh" ball, jump rope], storybooks.

GROUP SIZE: 30

TIME REQUIRED: 50 minutes.

SPACE REQUIREMENTS: Classroom with breakout spaces for small task groups.

PREPARATION: Complete the assigned readings on the selection and implementation of program activities.

INSTRUCTIONS: Participate in the discussion of the readings as facilitated by the instructor. Raise the key points from your reading for further discussion and any questions and/or points you think need further exploration.

Read the instructions for the activity given below. Raise any questions or points needing clarification. Divide into task groups of 5-6 students each. Go to your group's designated breakout area to select a recorder to make the group's report during the class discussion. As a group, complete the activity according to the Instruction Sheet. The instructor will be available for consultation and will alert the groups with a "five minute warning" to prepare for the report to the whole group.

When your task group has completed the activity, reconvene in the classroom. The recorder for your task group will give the group's report when your group's turn comes. Participate in a brief critique of each activity as it is presented by each of the other task groups and in summarizing the key points learned from the activity.

PRACTITIONER'S NOTES:

- With what types of groups would you use this activity?

- At what stage(s) of group development would this activity be useful?

- How would member's characteristics, skills, and abilities influence the way you would modify and implement this activity?

- How would this activity contribute to the group goals, members' goals, and session goals?

- At what point in the group meeting would you introduce the activity?

- How would you evaluate the usefulness and impact of the activity on the group and its members?

Additional Suggested Readings:

Brandler, S. & Roman, C.P. (1991). *Group work skills and strategies for effective interventions* (pp. 128-131). Binghamton, NY: Haworth Press.

Middleman, R.R. (1968). A guide to the analysis of non-verbal content. In R.R. Middleman. *The non-verbal method in working with groups* (pp. 130-173). New York: Association Press.

Vinter, R.D. (1985). Program activities: An analysis of their effects on participant behavior. In M. Sundel, P. Glasser, R. Sarri, and R. Vinter. *Individual change through small groups (2ⁿᵈ ed.)* (pp. 226-236). New York: The Free Press.

Selecting and Implementing Group Work Activities – A Role-play

Instructions:

Task I: Each task group will select one type of activity material from those provided. The task group will evaluate the suitability of the selected activity in relation to the group and the situation described below. Based on your evaluation, choose and modify the activity best suited to the group, the stage of group development, and the group's goal(s).

In planning how to use the activity, decide how to use the materials and how to engage the group in doing the activity. Try to anticipate and address potential pitfalls (e.g., what is likely to happen if you choose to do finger painting with a group of children where some members have low impulse control; how could you make this activity "work" with this group?). Consider adaptations that might be needed (e.g., How would you change an active game for members using walkers or wheelchairs?)

Task II: Role-play the situation using the activity as you have modified it.

Task III: Choose a recorder/reporter. Critique the activity and discuss alternative ways of using this activity. Make notes on the critique for discussion during the report back time.

GROUP DESCRIPTION: The Flying Eagles is an afterschool group composed of ten fifth-graders (five boys and five girls) from the local public school. Two of the girls and one of the boys are very interested and adept at athletics. All but one of the group (the newest boy who joined the group in mid-October and who is a foster child who recently moved to the area to live with his new foster family) enjoys making things. It is now mid-November and the group has been meeting every afternoon after school since September. Most of the group was together last year as well. The theme for the month focuses on harvest time and the Thanksgiving holiday.

As the field intern assigned to co-lead this group with a BSW practitioner, you are responsible for designing this session's activity. The activity should last 15 minutes. It follows the check-in circle and the snack the group has as part of the daily routine. After the activity, the group has free choice time for 1/2 an hour. The remainder of the session (usually about an hour) is spent on homework or reading before the bus comes to take them home.

ACTIVITY 1-13: Team Chowder: A Recipe for a Successful Task Group

IN THE CLASSROOM: *Team Chowder* will assist you and your group in discussing expectations for participation in class.

IN THE FIELD: In your practice you can use *Team Chowder* or one of its variations with groups of small children with sufficient verbal skills to participate. As the group worker, you may choose to write the recipe and illustrate each ingredient with drawings or pictures from a magazine. You might also post the recipe in the meeting area as a colorful reminder of the group norms. *Friendship Stew* developed by Susan Ciardiello in her work with latency age children is the model for *Team Chowder.* Her goal was to "help the children identify their own needs as well as the needs of others in friendship." The children would write down the recipe to take home to "practice with siblings and friends." She asked the children to draw a picture or write about their experience during the week in using an ingredient from the recipe (Ciardiello, S. (1999). *I Play, You Play, We All Play Together: Using Group Activities to Promote Resiliency in Latency Age Children,* an unpublished manuscript).

You can also use this activity in the preaffiliation stage of group development with groups of older children through adults and for staff in-service training, group supervision groups, and professional development workshops. You can adapt *Team Chowder* to various issues in group development and /or member behavior, using it as a vehicle to promote discussion about key elements of interpersonal activities (e.g., *Staff Soup*, ingredients that make a good colleague, as a topic for a staff supervision group in the power and control stage of group development).

MATERIALS: 6 large bowls, 90 strips of colorful paper, 1-4 markers per group, one flip chart sheet with one thick marker per group, additional newsprint to use under the flip chart as a blotter to protect the writing space, masking tape.

GROUP SIZE: 30 (six task groups with five members each)

TIME REQUIRED: 30 minutes—five minutes to introduce the activity; 10 minutes to create the chowder; 15 minutes to report back on the recipes.

SPACE REQUIREMENTS: Classroom with six small breakout meeting spaces; enough wall space in the classroom to post the task group's recipes.

PREPARATION: The instructor will gather the materials and equipment listed above, arrange the room and the breakout spaces to support the activity, and will prepare the wall space for posting the recipes.

INSTRUCTIONS: Before you break into smaller task groups, listen as the instructor introduces the activity and explains the goal. In the preliminary discussion, you will have an opportunity to contribute some ideas about what is needed for task groups to function effectively. Be specific and clear about your expectations for yourself and others in working together on future tasks. The following includes the basic instructions for the activity; your instructor may choose to make some changes for your particular class. When you have listened to the instructions, raise any questions you may have and ask for clarification of any areas that are unclear to you. Form the task groups, and distribute the materials for the activity to the groups. Your instructor will be available for consultation as needed. You will have 10 minutes to complete the activity. Your instructor will alert the groups with a two-minute warning to finish your recipes.

Small Group Tasks: In the small group session, each group will select a recipe reporter. Then you will each select three slips of paper and write down one key ingredient for a well functioning task group on each slip without sharing your contributions with other members. Fold the slips and place them in the pot. When everyone has contributed three slips to the pot, the recipe recorder/reporter will ask each person to select an "ingredient" from the pot and read it aloud. The group should discuss any "ingredients" that raise issues for the group members before completing the final recipe. When the group is satisfied with each ingredient, the recorder adds it to the recipe in letters large and dark enough to be read easily across the classroom. [10 minutes]

Large Group Report Back: When your group has completed the task and the 10 minutes have elapsed, return to the classroom for the report back. Once the class has reconvened, the recorders will post the recipes on the wall or chalkboard. During the ensuing discussion, the recorders will describe their group's recipe and any significant points about how the recipe was developed. Be alert for similarities and differences among the recipes, for gaps in any of the recipes. The instructor will request volunteers from each group to type or email the recipes to the instructor who will reproduce the recipes for the groups. The recipes may be used as a basis for developing norms for your work together as on-going task groups.

PRACTITIONER'S NOTES:

- With what types of groups would you use this activity?

- At what stage(s) of group development would this activity be useful?

- How would member's characteristics, skills, and abilities influence the way you would modify and implement this activity?

- How would this activity contribute to the group goals, members' goals, and session goals?

- At what point in the group meeting would you introduce the activity?

- How would you evaluate the usefulness and impact of the activity on the group and its members?

Source: From *I Play, You Play, We All Play Together: Using Group Activities to Promote Resiliency in Latency Age Children,* an unpublished workshop packet by Susan Ciardiello, CSW, Catholic Guardian Society, New York, NY, presented at the 8th European Group Work, Symposium, London, August, 1999. This packet, with additional activities, is under contract with Mar-Co and has been adapted with permission of the publisher.

Chapter 2
Beginnings with Groups in Generalist Practice

BEGINNINGS WITH GROUPS IN GENERALIST PRACTICE

In this chapter you will encounter activities suited to the first two stages of group development, *preaffiliation* and *power and control*, and two activities that begin the transition to the third stage, *intimacy*. In the *preaffiliation stage of group development* (Garland, Jones, & Kolodny, 1973) group members begin the process of entering into new relationships with each other and with the group as a whole. Each participant in the group, worker and members alike, becomes known and begins to know others partly through the planned activities the worker includes in the group program and partly through the informal occurrences that surround the group's existence. As the group moves into encounters with other members and with the worker, the tasks of identifying and establishing one's place and role(s) in the group come into focus with the attendant work and sometimes struggles. Garland, Jones, and Kolodny (1973) call these phenomena the *power and control stage*. As the worker and the group members resolve these issues of power and control, the group becomes more cohesive and creates its own group identity. The group then moves on to the *intimacy stage* with the worker and the group members deepening relationships and revealing more about themselves. This evolution through the stages of group development does not happen automatically. The interventions the worker makes consciously with the group and the ways members interact with each other and with the worker have profound influences on the group. The worker's skillful selection and use of activities can foster positive growth and development for the group as a whole and for individual group members.

The fourteen activities in this section will help you, both in your role as student and later as a group worker, to learn about and work with aspects of the early stages of group development. One of the central assumptions of this manual is that the social work class is a socio-educational group that experiences the stages of group development in ways very similar to those experienced by groups in the practice setting. As you enter this class in the first few weeks of the semester, pay close attention to your own behavior, feelings, and thoughts and the behavior of other class members to see if you can discern indications typical of the *preaffiliation, power and control,* and *intimacy stages.* What you learn from these experiences can be helpful in gaining empathy for the feelings and behaviors you encounter with the members of your groups in your field placement or in your later professional practice and guide your ways of being with and intervening in the group.

The first six activities (A 2-1 through A 2-6) are variations on traditional icebreakers often used in the initial session to help group members get to know and remember each other's names. Barker (1995, p. 177) defines ice breakers as "…the activities originated by group leaders in the *preaffiliation stage of group development* to create a comforting and productive atmosphere and become usefully acquainted with one another." Since groups first met in the early settlement houses, virtually every group worker has devised some type of game to help members learn each other's names. Some of these activities also help you to discover additional information about members' likes/dislikes and their unique experiences. This data will assist you in making a preliminary assessment of group members and the group as a whole.

Activities A 2-7 *Student Data Sheet*, A 2-8 *Forming Groups*, and A 2-9 *Creating Group Norms* will move the class from the fun and games of the icebreakers into a reflective phase designed to lay the foundation for your work together. In engaging in these activities, you will consider what you bring to the class (*Student Data Sheet, Forming Groups*) and accept responsibility as a class member for the way the class will function (*Creating Group Norms*). At this stage, you may begin to notice some of the phenomena associated with the *power and control stage of group development*. As you observe your own behavior and that of class members and the instructor, consider who raises challenges, who accepts challenges, and how the members interact with each other. Also consider how the instructor interacts with the class and individual members at this point in the semester.

The next three activities, A 2-10 *Structured Conversations,* A 2-11 *Respect in the Diverse Group,* and A 2-12 *Learning Climate Analysis,* address issues sometimes associated with the *power and control stage.* In *Structured Conversations*, class members begin the process of self-revelation in pairs using conversational topics formalized in the *Conversations* booklet. You will move to form new pairs with each successive topic, thus expanding your acquaintance with group members. This activity offers a way for class members to get to know something more about each other in a structured way and encourages you to use active listening skills. It may also challenge and reduce prejudices that you may have had about some class members. Teaching colleagues and I have even used both *Respect in the Diverse Group,* and *Learning Climate Analysis* effectively in classes where students have had difficulty in forming productive relationships with each other, though neither activity should be limited to dealing with such dilemmas. *Respect in the Diverse Group* helps the class to raise difficult issues in a structured and controlled way and encourages healthy resolution of the problems where they may exist. Similarly the *Learning Climate Analysis* can assist class members to broaden their assessment of each other's skills and abilities and foster a positive working environment in the classroom.

The last two activities will begin the class's transition into the *intimacy stage*, establishing a reflective mode that fosters a deepening of the working relationships in the class. In A 2-14 *The Reflecting Pool*, the emphasis is on a metaphoric exploration of the attributes each member brings to the class and how the class as a whole grows and changes with each member's contribution. In A 2-13 *A Letter to Myself*, each member sets out their hopes, fears, and expectations for participation in the class, and in exchanging letters with another class member, makes a commitment to the group. Each of these activities foreshadows the next stage of group development, *differentiation*, the stage where the group reaches its optimum work level. In this case this is the point where the class begins a concerted effort to accomplish the educational goals they have developed for themselves and those that the social work program has developed for degree candidates.

All activities in this section include approaches for using the classroom activity in practice situations either in the field practicum or in your later professional employment. In fact, each of the icebreakers and A 2-9 *Creating Group Norms* have all been drawn directly from professional practice with groups of children, youth, and young adults in settlement houses, community centers, and after-school programs. A 2-7 *Student Data Sheet* links with typical forms of data gathering used in group-serving agencies. The remaining activities originated as classroom experiential exercises but translate quite readily into the practice setting in ways suggested in the *In the Field* component of each activity. In addition to reading the connections to the field outlined in each activity, make sure to exercise your own creativity by using the Practitioner's Notes section to explore ways you can adapt these activities for the groups with whom you will be working. The most effective activities are developed in the context of your practice with the active participation of the group members in the process of selection, implementation, and evaluation. The more active the members are in taking responsibility and ownership for their group in a positive way, the more productive and effective the group experience will be for everyone involved, members and worker alike.

References:

Barker, R.L. (1995). *The social work dictionary (3rd ed.).* Washington, DC: NASW.

Garland, J.A., Jones, H.E. and Kolodny, R.L. (1973). A model for stages of development in social work groups. In S. Bernstein (Ed.). *Explorations in group work: Essays in theory and practice.* (pp. 17-71). Boston, MA: Milford House Inc.

ACTIVITY 2-1: Paired Introductions

IN THE CLASSROOM: *Paired Introductions* gives you an opportunity to use your interviewing skills, provides a way to learn classmates' names, and helps you to begin getting acquainted with class members.

IN THE FIELD: Similarly, when you use *Paired Introductions* in your practice, your purpose is to help group members become acquainted through a guided activity using questions relevant to the group's purpose. The questions you select should not probe into sensitive issues and should allow for some humor to surface. You can use this approach to introductions with any group where the members are able to carry on independent conversation.

MATERIALS: Blackboard and chalk or newsprint and marker. Individual printed interview sheets may facilitate the activity in larger groups.

GROUP SIZE: Up to 30

TIME REQUIRED: 15 to 45 minutes, depending on group size

SPACE REQUIREMENTS: Sufficient space between pairs to allow for conversation without too much distraction from neighboring pairs. The space used should allow for students to be seated in a circle initially and for the pairs to move around and to find a comfortable location to talk with each other with a minimum of furniture moving.

INSTRUCTIONS: Find a partner to interview. If you already know some or all of the class members, find someone to interview that you don't know very well. Select three items from the Topics List below. You have six minutes to complete the two interviews. Ask the instructor if you need clarification of the instructions, then proceed with the interviews. After the allotted interviewing time, volunteer to make the introductions at the appropriate time. Listen carefully as class members introduce each other. This information will be useful to you as you develop your professional network.

Classroom Interview Topics:

· Describe your field placement. What do you like best/least about your placement?

· Tell me something about you that no one at school knows about you.

· What is your favorite way to spend spring break?

· What is the most adventurous thing you have ever done?

· Tell me your most embarrassing moment.

· Why did you choose social work as your major?

PRACTITIONER'S NOTES:

· With what types of groups would you use this activity?

· At what stage(s) of group development would this activity be useful?

· How would member's characteristics, skills, and abilities influence the way you would modify and implement this activity? What topics would you use?

· How would this activity contribute to the group goals, members' goals, and session goals?

· At what point in the group meeting would you introduce the activity?

· How would you evaluate the usefulness and impact of the activity on the group and its members?

ACTIVITY 2-2: Going to Boston

IN THE CLASSROOM: *Going to Boston* is another icebreaker activity that will help you to learn and remember the names of your classmates.

IN THE FIELD: With groups in practice, name games serve as a low demand way to assist group members to learn each other's names and, depending on the variation, to learn a bit about each other. As the game proceeds, participants near the middle and end of the activity have more names to remember. Keeping the game light and funny helps relieve the pressure on those who may forget a name or two and avoid hurt feeling for those whose names may be harder to remember.

You can vary the basic game in a number of ways. The Name Game variation proceeds with participants attaching an adjective beginning with their first initial of their names (e.g., Musical Marcia, Distinguished David). In the Likes version participants add information about a preference beginning with the first initial of their names (e.g., Hi, I'm Marcia and I like munchies. Hi, I'm David and I like dinosaurs. This is Marcia and she likes munchies.). These games may help both the members and the group worker remember names through the mnemonic devices.

MATERIALS: None

GROUP SIZE: 30 maximum

TIME REQUIRED: 5-15 minutes, depending on group size

SPACE REQUIREMENTS: Enough space for students to be seated comfortably in a circle.

INSTRUCTIONS: When everyone is seated in the circle, the first student will say her/his name and the destination (e.g., "Hi, my name is Susan and I am going to Boston."). The next student says his/her name, the destination and the names of their travelling companions (e.g., "Hi, my name is Jim. I am going to Boston with Susan." And the next students continue the process, adding in the names of all the previous players. The activity continues until the last student has introduced her/himself and repeated in sequence the names of all the "traveling companions" who introduced themselves earlier.

PRACTITIONER'S NOTES:

·   With what types of groups would you use this activity?

·   At what stage(s) of group development would this activity be useful?

·   How would member's characteristics, skills, and abilities influence the way you would modify and implement this activity?

· How would this activity contribute to the group goals, members' goals, and session goals?

· At what point in the group meeting would you introduce the activity?

· How would you evaluate the usefulness and impact of the activity on the group and its members?

Source: The Name Game was contributed by Marcia Cohen, PhD, Professor, University of New England School of Social Work, Portland, ME.

ACTIVITY 2-3: Beanbag Toss

IN THE CLASSROOM: *Beanbag Toss* is a more active approach to help you reinforce learning your classmates' names. It will also energize the class through movement.

IN THE FIELD: You can use the *Beanbag Toss* with young children through teens in the preaffiliation phase of group development. As in the classroom version, this activity provides reinforcement after a preliminary activity where group members have already introduced themselves to the group. For younger children's groups you might use a beanbag shaped like an animal. Frogs are good because they can "jump" from participant to participant. You might introduce the animal beanbag by name (e.g., Freddie the Frog) and create a short story about how Freddie wants to get to know everyone's name. You can remind the group that Freddie the Frog doesn't like to jump too quickly or land too hard, thus limiting potential damage to either Freddie or the children participating.

MATERIALS: Small beanbag or other small, soft object that can be tossed safely without bouncing away.

GROUP SIZE: Up to 30

TIME REQUIRED: 5 – 30 minutes depending on group size and capabilities.

SPACE REQUIRMENTS: A space large enough to form a circle (in chairs, seated on the floor, or standing) comfortably for the size of the class.

INSTRUCTIONS: The goal of the game is to remember each other's names. The first student who has the beanbag says, "My name is... and I am tossing the beanbag to..." If the first student names the recipient correctly, the recipient selects a new person to receive the beanbag using the same verbal formula. If the first student names the recipient incorrectly, the recipient tosses the beanbag back saying, "My name is... and I am tossing the beanbag back to..." and the student tries again. The game proceeds until everyone has had a turn or the instructor determines it is time to end the game.

PRACTITIONER'S NOTES:

· With what types of groups would you use this activity?

· At what stage(s) of group development would this activity be useful?

· How would member's characteristics, skills, and abilities influence the way you would modify and implement this activity?

· How would this activity contribute to the group goals, members' goals, and session goals?

· At what point in the group meeting would you introduce the activity?

· How would you evaluate the usefulness and impact of the activity on the group and its members?

ACTIVITY 2-4: Name Search

IN THE CLASSROOM: The *Name Search* is a pencil and paper activity that will help you to remember classmates' names.

IN THE FIELD: The *Name Search* is useful as a follow-up activity to help group members to remember each other's names. Beyond the preaffiliation stage, you can modify the activity in several ways. For example, rather than using names you can create a *Word Search* puzzle adapted to various session topics by using key words that will trigger reactions or discussion about their meanings and significance or by using terms from assigned readings. For example, with youth in a babysitter-training program or teen mothers in a parenting support group you might use words denoting aspects of childcare (i.e., play, discipline, fantasy, safety, tantrum, naptime, swing, diapers). Note that *The Name Search* and any of its variations require that the group members have some facility with spelling and enough eye-hand coordination to recognize and circle the letters in the puzzle. The task can be simplified by adding a name or word list to the puzzle. To reduce the difficulty of the puzzle, avoid words written backwards and/or diagonally.

MATERIALS: Puzzle sheets, table or clipboards for completing the puzzle, prepared solutions.

GROUP SIZE: Up to 30

TIME REQUIRED: 10 – 30 minutes.

SPACE REQUIREMENTS: Sufficient table space for the class members to complete the puzzle conveniently.

PREPARATION: Before the next class session, use the Instruction Sheet below puzzle using the class list that you have gathered in the Get Acquainted activity earlier. With the longest name among the class members as a base word, build the puzzle by linking names to the base work and building the puzzle by inserting additional names horizontally, vertically, backwards, forwards, and diagonally. You can also have two names use some of the same letters. See EXAMPLE 1 below in which the puzzle is built from the base word, *CHRISTINA*.

EXAMPLE 1: *Sample Class List:* Christina, Diana, Dodi, Gloria, Lisa, Lou, Marilyn, Meg, Milli, Robin, Rob, Sheila, Tim [Note how Dodi and Diana use two of the same letters.]

```
            M           L
D O D I A N A       I
            R           S
G C H R I S T I N A
L   I L L I M   M —
O       Y       I   U
R O B I N   T   O
I                   L
A L I E H S   M E G
```

Next, fill in the spaces with random letters as shown in EXAMPLE 2. If you are using a word processor to print the final version, use a font that does not use variable spacing (e.g., Courier works well).

EXAMPLE 2:

```
L O G S M A R T G L
D O D I A N A E C I
T I N M R S I T O S
G C H R I S T I N A
L S I L L I M E M O
O U S N Y O N I R U
R O B I N X T U S O
I A B C D E A G H L
A L I E H S A M E G
```

Also make a solution sheet as shown in EXAMPLE 3. Bring your puzzle and solution sheet to the next class.

EXAMPLE 3: *Solution Sheet*

```
L O G S M A R T G L
D O D I A N A E C I
T I N M R S I T O S
G C H R I S T I N A
L S I L L I M E M O
O U S N Y O N I R U
R O B I N X T U S O
I A B C D E A G H L
A L I E H S A M E G
```

INSTRUCTIONS: **In class you will find a partner and exchange your puzzles. In the next five minutes try to solve your partner's puzzle without using the Solution Sheet. When you have finished the puzzle, swap the Solution Sheets to see how well you have done. Then the class will participate in a discussion of the activity facilitated by the instructor. Contribute to the discussion by commenting on your reactions to the activity. Consider what techniques made the puzzles easier or harder for you? Speculate on ways you might modify the activity for particular groups.**

PRACTITIONER'S NOTES:

·   With what types of groups would you use this activity?

·   At what stage(s) of group development would this activity be useful?

·   How would member's characteristics, skills, and abilities influence the way you would modify and implement this activity?

- How would this activity contribute to the group goals, members' goals, and session goals?

- At what point in the group meeting would you introduce the activity?

- How would you evaluate the usefulness and impact of the activity on the group and its members?

NAME SEARCH

Instructions

1. During the Get Acquainted time, your task is to learn everyone's name and to get the correct spelling. Use the space at the bottom of puzzle sheet to record the names.

2. In the space marked *Name Search Puzzle*, create a word puzzle using the names of each member of the class. You may write the names forwards, backwards, diagonally, vertically, or horizontally.

3. When you have finished the puzzle, make a *Solution Sheet* with the names highlighted.

4. In the next class session, bring the puzzle to swap with a class member. Solve your partner's puzzle by circling as many names as you can find in the puzzle.

NAME SEARCH PUZZLE

Created by: _____

ACTIVITY 2-5: Investigation

IN THE CLASSROOM: *Investigation* will promote class interaction and help you and the other class members get to know a bit about each other.

IN THE FIELD: You can use this activity with groups from school age through adult. You will need to develop topic areas that are relevant to the group's composition and purpose. You can expand *Investigation* with additional topics, depending on the amount of time available for the activity. For example, in the classroom setting, Marcia Cohen, PhD, of University of New England (UNE) School of Social Work uses these additional items:

· Was born outside New England

· Drives a foreign car

· Travels more than 50 miles (one way) to get to UNE

· Owns a dog

· Has more than three siblings

· Plays a musical instrument

· Has traveled to a continent other than North America

· Speaks a language other than English

You might give small, joke prizes to members with the most items completed, for other items included on the sheet (e.g., the person born the farthest away, the most embarrassing of the embarrassing moments reported), or to everyone for being good sports. Where members have varying degrees of mobility, make sure you have enough space for them to maneuver wheel chairs or walkers so the activity runs smoothly. For members with sight or vision restrictions, conducting the exercise in teams of two or three offers an alternate way to complete the activity.

MATERIALS: Pencils, activity sheet.

GROUP SIZE: 30 maximum

TIME REQUIRED: 20 minutes

SPACE REQUIREMENTS: Sufficient space for mingling.

INSTRUCTIONS: Read the Instruction Sheet below. You will have ten minutes to complete your *Investigation* by finding individuals who fit the description for each of the items listed. Make sure to spell each person's first and last name correctly. You may only use one name per item, without duplicating any names. A one-minute warning will signal that time will be up for completing the activity. Take your seat and report your findings when your turn comes.

PRACTITIONER'S NOTES:

· With what types of groups would you use this activity?

· At what stage(s) of group development would this activity be useful?

· How would member's characteristics, skills, and abilities influence the way you would modify and implement this activity?

· How would this activity contribute to the group goals, members' goals, and session goals?

· At what point in the group meeting would you introduce the activity?

· How would you evaluate the usefulness and impact of the activity on the group and its members?

INVESTIGATION

Instructions: In the next five minutes, find someone in the class who fits each of the descriptions below. Write that person's first and last name spelled correctly, in the blank space next to the item. Use each name only once.

1. Someone who was born outside of this state:

_____

2. Someone who has done volunteer work:

_____

3. Someone who lives in this town:

_____

4. Someone who has an unusual hobby:

_____

5. Someone who will tell you their most embarrassing experience:

_____

ACTIVITY 2-6: Who Are Your Neighbors?

IN THE CLASSROOM: *Who are Your Neighbors* is a game that will help to reinforce remembering classmates' names. The movement aspects also help to energize the class.

IN THE FIELD: *Who Are Your Neighbors* is a useful icebreaker in the preaffiliation stage of group development or energizer in the intimacy phase with groups from school-age children and youth. Use caution in using this activity in the power and control stage as the follow-up question, "how do you like your neighbors," may encourage unpleasantness. You could drop the second question. This activity may be used with adults depending on their willingness to engage in light-hearted game playing. It is best used with groups that have enough large muscle control to manage quick seat changes without sustaining injury.

MATERIALS: One chair fewer than the number of students.

GROUP SIZE: 6-30

TIME REQUIRED: 5-10 minutes, depending on group size and enthusiasm for game playing.

SPACE REQUIREMENTS: Enough space to form a circle of chairs with a large space in the center for changing seats.

PREPARATION: Arrange the chairs in a circle. The class should have already done an initial activity for class members to learn each other's names.

INSTRUCTIONS: When everyone is seated in the circle, remind the persons seated to your right and left of your name. The instructor will request a volunteer to be the first Questioner. The first Questioner will choose the first Responder and ask the Responder, "Who are your neighbors?" If the Responder answers incorrectly, the Questioner takes the Responder's seat, and Responder becomes the new Questioner. If the Responder answers correctly, the Questioner then asks, "How do you like your neighbors?" The Responder can say, "Very much" or "Not at all." If the answer is "very much," the Questioner moves on to another Responder and repeats the process. If the answer is "not at all," everyone changes seats, with the Questioner trying to get a seat. Whoever is left without a seat becomes the next Questioner. The game proceeds until most participants have had a turn to be the Questioner.

PRACTITIONER'S NOTES:

·   With what types of groups would you use this activity?

·   At what stage(s) of group development would this activity be useful?

·   How would member's characteristics, skills, and abilities influence the way you would modify and implement this activity?

·   How would this activity contribute to the group goals, members' goals, and session goals?

·   At what point in the group meeting would you introduce the activity?

How would you evaluate the usefulness and impact of the activity on the group and its members?

ACTIVITY 2-7: Student Data Sheet

IN THE CLASSROOM: The *Student Data Sheet* will help you to focus your attention on this new classroom experience and on the way it fits in with your past experiences. It will facilitate your reflection on your goals for participation in this class and the activities to come.

IN THE FIELD: You can use similar *Participant Data* forms with items relevant to the purpose of the group with both task and treatment groups that you facilitate in your practice. For example, in a parenting education group for teen parents, you might ask group members to identify any previous child care experience (e.g., babysitting, caring for siblings), courses taken at school or a social agency (e.g., babysitter training at the Y), best group experience, worst group experience, goals for participating in this group, what they most want to avoid in this group experience. Well before the meeting where you use this activity, you will need to duplicate sufficient copies, one per group member plus a few extras in case of spoilage. Completing the Data Sheet requires a basic level of reading and writing skill. In situations where group members may be unable to complete the sheet, the worker can gather the data in pre-group interviews and report the aggregate information to the group as part of developing norms and group goals.

MATERIALS: Data sheets, one per student; pencils.

GROUP SIZE: Unlimited, 30 optimum.

TIME REQUIRED: 15 minutes

SPACE REQUIREMENTS: A meeting space with writing space for each student to complete the Data Sheet with some privacy.

INSTRUCTIONS: This activity focuses on the ways past learning experiences—positive, negative, and neutral—have impact on expectations we bring to each new experience. The items on the Data Sheet will help raise some of the key issues for reflection and discussion with the whole class. Before the activity begins, the instructor may ask you to talk about experiences that have influenced your career choice and goals. Once you have the Data Sheets and a pencil, take ten minutes to complete the form. The instructor will collect the forms. Before the next session, the instructor will review and aggregate the data that will be shared with the class. This follow-up discussion will be used to lead into the development of group goals, objectives, and norms for the class.

After you have completed the Data Sheet, the instructor may ask you to meet in small groups to discuss items that will lead into the creation of group norms and/or goals. Each group will, then, select their three most important norms and three goals for the class's work together. During the report back, you will contribute these items to the discussion and creation of norms/goals for the class.

PRACTITIONER'S NOTES:

·   With what types of groups would you use this activity?

·   At what stage(s) of group development would this activity be useful?

· How would member's characteristics, skills, and abilities influence the way you would modify and implement this activity?

· How would this activity contribute to the group goals, members' goals, and session goals?

· At what point in the group meeting would you introduce the activity?

· How would you evaluate the usefulness and impact of the activity on the group and its members?

STUDENT DATA SHEET

Name: _____   Address: _____

Phone: [h]_____ [w]_____Email: _____

Previous Course Related Experiences:

Course Related Personal Interests:

Career Goals:

Course Attitudes, Expectations, Goals:

Worst Classroom Experience:

Best Classroom Experience:

ACTIVITY 2-8: Forming Groups – Experience/Knowledge Self Assessment

IN THE CLASSROOM: Multiple ways to create working groups exist. This activity will help you to explore one approach to group formation for discussion groups and focus your attention on the importance of this aspect of social work practice with groups.

IN THE FIELD: This exercise works well with in-service training groups. It makes concrete the respect that you as the trainer have for the diversity of knowledge and experience that participants bring to the training. Furthermore, when groups are composed homogeneously on these two dimensions, the exercise helps to create task groups that have some significant commonality from the start. In planning for this activity, you will need to prepare the transparency or slide before the session or create the format on the chalkboard or newsprint in the session. Other dimensions may be used to replace knowledge/experience, depending on the purpose of the training and the small groups.

To reduce group members' concerns about sharing information on sensitive topics with the whole group, you can ask group members to comment on the examples before beginning the self-assessment, noting areas that may be too intrusive. Be alert to body language as well as the nuances of verbal responses. Request help from the group in reworking the examples to make them more useful in forming the groups. If the exercise is too stressful for group members, it may be wise to abandon this method of group formation for the particular topic area.

Occasionally group members may over- or under-estimate their knowledge/experience levels. An inaccurate self-assessment may be most problematic when the exercise is used to form homogeneous groups. If the groups will be ongoing over a period of weeks, you should inform groups that some changes in the group composition may be necessary during the first two weeks to improve the efficacy and functioning of the groups.

MATERIALS: Blackboard, chalk; newsprint, markers; overhead projector and transparency; or Power Point slide.

GROUP SIZE: 30-40

TIME REQUIRED: 10 minutes

SPACE REQUIREMENTS: Classroom with breakout spaces for resulting small groups to hold discussion.

PREPARATION: Each member of the class brings a wealth of already acquired knowledge and experience to the classroom. Both your knowledge and experience will be important factors in shaping how your new learning will take place. Consider what you have learned from your Human Behavior in the Social Environment courses about work done on learning schema and cognitive processes in cognitive development theory, particularly by Piaget. Also consider what you have learned about groups, especially the importance of purposeful group composition as an essential element in creating productive groups.

Review the purpose, goals, and objectives for the small groups that will be formed using the knowledge/experience grid. Be prepared to give examples that make the key variables concrete for each of the four cells. Specific examples clearly related to the topic for small group discussion will help you begin to understand ways to evaluate your knowledge base and your level of experience realistically. Focus your examples on actual, personal knowledge and experience, not on opinions. However, you should not feel pressured to share highly charged personal experiences (i.e., previous substance abuse, chronic illness, controversial health decisions).

INSTRUCTIONS: Using the grid presented below, assess your experience and knowledge base in relation to the planned small group activity or discussion topic. Depending on the goal of the exercise and the time available, the instructor may ask you to report your self-classification and the way you reached your decision or ask the class to begin the task group session with a discussion of members' decision making processes. Depending on the purpose of the small group discussion, the instructor will ask the class to divide into four groups either homogeneously or heterogeneously based on your self-assessments. If any category has only one person, that person should join with the group that approximates her/his knowledge/experience range most closely. If the whole group is very large, some of the groups for one or more of the four categories may exceed seven members. In this case, the class will divide these larger groups into sub-groups, with a minimum of three and a maximum of seven members in each sub-group.

SELF ASSESSMENT GRID

LOW KNOWLEDGE, LOW EXPERIENCE	HIGH KNOWLEDGE, LOW EXPERIENCE
LOW KNOWLEDGE, HIGH EXPERIENCE	HIGH KNOWLEDGE, HIGH EXPERIENCE

When the small group session is concluded, you will reconvene as a class for a report-back and follow-up discussion so that the whole group can benefit from the full range of knowledge and experience that emerges from the small task groups. In closing reflect on your observations of the method and outcome of the process of group composition, noting where there are clusters of demographic variables such as gender, race, age, ethnicity, etc. Explore the expected and unexpected occurrences. Link your observations to what you know about strategies for group composition.

PRACTITIONER'S NOTES:

·   With what types of groups would you use this activity?

·   At what stage(s) of group development would this activity be useful?

·   How would member's characteristics, skills, and abilities influence the way you would modify and implement this activity?

·   How would this activity contribute to the group goals, members' goals, and session goals?

·   At what point in the group meeting would you introduce the activity?

·   How would you evaluate the usefulness and impact of the activity on the group and its members?

Source: From Thompson, M.E. (1993). Building groups on students' knowledge and experience. *Teaching Sociology, 21*(1), 96. Adapted with permission.

ACTIVITY 2-9: Creating Group Norms

IN THE CLASSROOM: This activity facilitates your work with classmates to create the working norms for the class in a positive way. It also models a participatory learning and teaching style and engages class members in taking responsibility for their share of the work of the task group and the class.

IN THE FIELD: In your practice you can use *Creating Group Norms* with groups of young children through adults. With young children, the number of norms should not exceed five or six simple rules, positively stated. Printing the norms on a colorful poster with artwork created by the children and keyed to illustrate each rule helps remind the group of the ground rules. A similar approach works well with older children and teens. In adult groups the approach used in the classroom exercise works well. For some groups where it is helpful to have the norms visible during sessions, you can post the working document on a large sign in the meeting room. Creating and decorating the Norms Poster could be another group activity. Alternatively, if the group has an on-line component, you can ask the recorder to post the norms on the site. When the norms have been created, remember to thank the group for their participation and the volunteers for their efforts.

MATERIALS: For session 1, flip chart and thick markers or blackboard and chalk; For session 2, one copy of the Norms working document for each student.

GROUP SIZE: 30-40 maximum.

TIME REQUIRED: 1 hour – 5 minutes for instructions, 20 minutes for small group discussion, 10-15 minutes for report back, 10 minutes to formulate the working document, plus time to move between classroom and small group locations.

SPACE REQUIREMENTS: A classroom and enough breakout space to accommodate small groups.

INSTRUCTIONS: To create a constructive working climate in the classroom, you must phrase norms positively. To begin this activity, the instructor will ask you to give examples of norms phrased positively by asking class members to rephrase "no" statements (e.g., "no hogging the floor in group discussion" could become "share the air time" or "give others opportunity to speak"). Some classroom norms are non-negotiable based on the instructor's usual practices and/or university rules.

Once the class has explored the activity, you will divide into small groups and will have 20 minutes to develop a list of proposed norms. Check with the instructor if you need clarification as the activity progresses. Each group will appoint a recorder who will present the group's list during the report back phase of the activity.

When the class reconvenes, a volunteer from the class will write the norms on the chalkboard using print large enough to be read from the back of the room. Look for similarities among the suggestions, and think about the best wording for each norm as the list evolves. Identify any norms that need clarification or with which you may disagree. Raise those issues for class discussion. After each group has made their presentation, the class will discuss the proposed norms and develop the final document. A volunteer from the class will copy the final document and give it to the instructor for duplication and distribution to the class. The class norms are a "work in progress." Class members can request that the norms be revisited if changes need to be made. Keep your copy of the norms with your class notes and review it periodically.

PRACTITIONER'S NOTES:

·   With what types of groups would you use this activity?

·   At what stage(s) of group development would this activity be useful?

·   How would member's characteristics, skills, and abilities influence the way you would modify and implement this activity?

·   How would this activity contribute to the group goals, members' goals, and session goals?

·   At what point in the group meeting would you introduce the activity?

·   How would you evaluate the usefulness and impact of the activity on the group and its members?

ACTIVITY 2-10: Structured Conversations

IN THE CLASSROOM: Participating in *Structured Conversations* will help you to get to know your classmates better. It will facilitate conversation and increase sharing of information.

IN THE FIELD: *Structured Conversations* can be used with school-age children through adults by varying the topic pages to suit both the reading levels of the group members and the purpose of the group and the session. Conversation starters may vary with group composition, purpose, and goal for the session. For example, with a group for children from divorced families, topics could raise issues that often concern children. Structuring the conversation around those topics may reduce isolation and address feelings of misplaced responsibility for the family's difficulties. *Structured Conversations* is an activity most often used in the preaffiliation stage of group development but could be used at any stage where communication has broken down, and you want a structured way to direct the interactions among group members. In the practice setting you will create booklets that have topic areas relevant to address the current situation occurring in the group. You can limit or expand the number of topics to fit the time available and the number of group members.

MATERIALS: A *Conversation* booklet for each member, pencils, a clock to time the conversation periods.

GROUP SIZE: Up to 30.

TIME REQUIRED: 15 – 45 minutes

SPACE REQUIREMENTS: Sufficient space to form a double line of students and space for the class to be seated in circle to discuss the activity after it is concluded. If the space does not permit using the pairs in two lines or if mobility issues are present, pairs may complete booklet pages without rotating.

PREPARATION: The instructor will be responsible for creating, duplicating, and assembling the booklets if the format below is not used.

INSTRUCTIONS: Review the questions in the booklet. Listen carefully to the instructor's directions about the way the activity will proceed. Raise any questions or points that you need to have clarified before the activity begins.

The class will form two lines facing each other at a distance comfortable for conversation. Each pair will change partners when they have completed their question by moving one space to the left with each new page of the *Conversation* booklet. If the class has an uneven number of members, use a spot at one end of the group as a rest stop or for the timekeeper's position. As the pairs change, the student without a partner may either rest or assume the timekeeper's role, watching the clock and calling for the next rotation to begin. In a group with even numbers, the instructor acts as a timekeeper. Each conversation will last three minutes.

When all the questions have been covered, you will take your seat in a circle and discuss your reactions to the activity and any surprises that may have emerged in your conversations. Consider ways to vary the activity for groups with whom you are working in your field placement or in your employment.

PRACTITIONER'S NOTES:

· With what types of groups would you use this activity?

· At what stage(s) of group development would this activity be useful?

· How would member's characteristics, skills, and abilities influence the way you would modify and implement this activity?

· How would this activity contribute to the group goals, members' goals, and session goals?

· At what point in the group meeting would you introduce the activity?

· How would you evaluate the usefulness and impact of the activity on the group and its members?

Conversation Booklet

Instructions: With each new partner, turn to a new page in your booklet. Take turns sharing your views or comments on the topic printed on that page. Make sure to cover each topic in order without skipping topics.

Sample topic pages for a college or university classroom:

⊙   My favorite place on campus is….

⊙   On vacation I like to…

⊙   Quickly choose one of the following or fill in your own subject:

The first time I tried to [use a computer, use the stacks at the library, find my way to the social work bldg., performed before a group, or presented before a class], I….

⊙   If I could change universities, I would apply to

[Paraphrase your partner's response: "What I heard you say is…"]

⊙   Pick a topic from the last few pages that you would like to revisit; share that with this partner.

⊙   One quality I look for in a colleague is….

⊙   When I can have time alone, I….

[Give your partner some "impressions" as feedback: "You seem to be a person who…."

⊙   I came to this class because….

⊙   Three things I think I do very well are….

⊙   One thing about me that I would like to change is…

⊙   Tell your partner about a personal success that you have had and what it means to you….

⊙   A problem I am dealing with right now is….

⊙   Pick a topic from the last pages and ask your partner to tell you her/his view/comments on it.

⊙↘ Now that we have reached the last page in this booklet, I feel….

ACTIVITY 2-11: Respect in the Diverse Group

IN THE CLASSROOM: This activity offers you another way to consider your heritage and its impact on your work with clients and colleagues. It will help you to recognize similarities and differences among class members and to consider some sources of misunderstandings and potential/actual conflict. The ultimate goal for this activity is to develop respectful ways of interacting with each other to reduce potential or actual conflict and increase cooperation.

IN THE FIELD: You might use this activity with older school-age children, teens, and adult groups in situations where the purpose is to explore issues of diversity and respect or to confront circumstances where disrespect has arisen. You should be aware that finger pointing and blaming might accompany this activity if prior conflict has erupted. You can work to preempt these behaviors in the introduction of the activity by emphasizing that some conflict is a normal part of the life of most groups. Remind members of the norms they have already adopted. Reviewing the norms will help set the ground rules for working together in the small groups.

MATERIALS: Instruction sheet, pencil, and paper for each student

GROUP SIZE: 30 maximum

TIME REQUIRED: Approximately 1 Ω hours

SPACE REQUIREMENTS: A classroom with enough breakout areas for small groups to have some privacy in their discussion.

PREPARATION: Read the instruction sheets and raise any questions and points needing clarification.

INSTRUCTIONS: Divide into small groups. Each group will select a recorder/reporter. In the next 40 minutes, complete the activities listed on the instruction sheet. The groups will take a 10-minute break and then resume for a 20-minute discussion.

PRACTITIONER'S NOTES:

· With what types of groups would you use this activity?

· At what stage(s) of group development would this activity be useful?

· How would member's characteristics, skills, and abilities influence the way you would modify and implement this activity?

· How would this activity contribute to the group goals, members' goals, and session goals?

·   At what point in the group meeting would you introduce the activity?

·   How would you evaluate the usefulness and impact of the activity on the group and its members?

RESPECT IN THE DIVERSE GROUP

Small Group Discussion

Instructions: Select a reporter. Complete the following activities in order and within the time limits indicated. When all the activities have been addressed, take a 10-minute break, returning to the classroom at the designated time.

1. Using the paper and pencils provided, write a short paragraph about your name/ nickname, the meaning(s), the story of how you got them, and how you relate to your name(s). Share the information with the group. Decide what would be useful for the class to know. The reporter will prepare and bring that information back to the class. [15 min.]

2. Next you will give the group information about your ethnicity and background, paying attention to the similarities and diversity among group members. As a group, summarize the findings for the report to the class. [15 min.]

3. The group will move on to discuss how each group member perceives respect, building a base for work together as members of the class and as members of class task groups. Prepare a brief statement from the group for the reporter to bring to the class. [20 min.]

4. Class discussion of each group's experience. [20 min.]

Source: Adapted from Getting Started: Respect Exercise and Name Stories from *Multicultural Pavilion Awareness Activities.*

Retrieved from http://curry.edschool.virginia.edu/go/multicultural/home.html and adapted with permission.

ACTIVITY 2-12: Learning Climate Analysis

IN THE CLASSROOM: The *Learning Climate Analysis* activity will help you and the members of your task group to assess aspects of trust within your group and to consider the impact of the trust levels on the work of your groups and the class as a whole.

IN THE FIELD: You might use the *Learning Climate Analysis* with task groups of older youth through adults to prevent or identify problem areas in group functioning and to suggest ways to enhance group functioning. You might choose to use the activity in the power and control stage and then revisit it periodically to assist in maintaining effective group functioning. In groups experiencing problems related to trust and members' functioning, keeping the focus on the positive characteristics used in the analysis form helps to prevent further erosion of trust and behavior. When introducing the activity, you may also wish to review norms that the group has developed to help set the context for assessing member roles. Where groups have been experiencing difficulties, it is important for you to be available for consultation with task groups during the exercise and to check in with the groups periodically to monitor progress.

MATERIALS: A *Learning Climate Analysis* form given at the end of these instructions—one per student, pencils, and tables, desks, or writing boards. Newsprint, markers, and tape for posting the results.

GROUP SIZE: Up to 30

TIME REQUIRED: 50 minutes

SPACE REQUIREMENTS: Classroom with breakout spaces for small group discussion to occur with a minimum of interruption.

PREPARATION: Review the instructions on the *Learning Climate Analysis* form and raise any points that need clarification.

INSTRUCTIONS: The type of assessment you will do in this activity is designed to help increase the effectiveness of your task group and the class as a whole in meeting group and individual goals. It will help you to identify members' strengths and to address perceptions and misperceptions among group members. As the level of trust among group members increases, you each will be able to participate in the group's work more positively and effectively and the need to use unproductive behavior and strategies that members may be using [i.e., defensiveness, manipulation] will diminish.

Divide into your task groups, taking with you newsprint, markers, and tape for making the list you will post for the concluding discussion. The instructor will be available for consultation during the process and will check in with groups periodically. You will have 40 minutes to complete the form and hold the discussion. Each task group will post their selections when the class reconvenes, and the class will participate in a concluding discussion of the last item in the instructions, the recommendations for increasing trust levels.

To complete the forms, you will link your selections with experiences you have had in classroom activities that substantiate your choices. The group members will need to reach consensus on the selections in your group. As the discussion progresses, make sure that you discuss your reactions to the selection the group makes for each of you. Also consider the impact of member roles on the work of your task group and the class as a whole.

When the instructor reconvenes the class, your group will post your newsprint consensus list in the space allocated to your group. Each group will report their recommendations for increasing trust levels. The instructor will facilitate a discussion of the class members' reactions, surprises, or comments that may arise from participating in the activity. Each group should plan ways to incorporate the results of the activity into their future interactions with both the task groups and the class. Also consider specific ways you might use this activity in your field setting. This approach will help you to transfer what you have experienced by participating in this activity to your work in your field placement and your professional practice.

PRACTITIONER'S NOTES:

·   At what stage(s) of group development would this activity be useful?

·   How would member's characteristics, skills, and abilities influence the way you would modify and implement this activity?

·   How would this activity contribute to the group goals, members' goals, and session goals?

·   At what point in the group meeting would you introduce the activity?

·   How would you evaluate the usefulness and impact of the activity on the group and its members?

Source: From Nominations: Personal Instrumented Feedback in W.J. Pfeiffer and J.E. Jones, (Eds). *A handbook for structured experiences in human relations training*, pp. 33-38. Copyright 1974 by Pfeiffer & Co. This material is used by permission of Pfeiffer/Jossey-Bass, Inc., a subsidiary of John Wiley & Sons, Inc.

Learning Climate Analysis Form

Instructions:

1. Read each definition.

2. Select the member you think most closely resembles the definition.

3. When everyone is finished, compare nominations for each definition.

4. Come to a group consensus on the one person who most fits each definition.

5. Post the selections on the newsprint.

6. Consider ways to increase the trust level; prepare report for the larger group.

Definitions: A person may be said to be...

1. **AWARE** when her/his outward behavior reflects inner feelings and thoughts, when the person recognizes explicitly how feelings are influencing behavior; when the person recognizes and responds to those feelings. Awareness may be indicated by a statement such as "I feel somewhat at a loss, we don't have a topic" (instead of "We're just floundering without something we can get our teeth into").

Your nomination_____ Consensus_____

2. **SELF-ACCEPTING** when the person can accept her/his own feelings without denying them, giving rationalizations for them, or apologizing for them. Self-acceptance may be evidenced by a statement such as "I'm angry at myself for being so ineffective with this issue" (instead of "This group is not getting anywhere").

Your nomination_____ Consensus_____

3. **ACCEPTING OF OTHERS** when the person is able to accept the feelings and thoughts of others without trying to change them; when the person is able to let others be themselves even though they are different for her/him: Acceptance of others may be shown by listening in order to understand; by listening without trying to refute; by trying not to argue; by asking questions in order to understand; or by not judging another.

Your nomination_____ Consensus_____

4. **SUPPORTIVE** when the person seeks to help others reach goals that are important to them, when the person tries to understand what others want to do although she/he may not agree with their conclusions; or when the person encourages others to try behavior new to them.

Your nomination_____ Consensus_____

5. **RISK-TAKING** when the person goes beyond the known by experimenting with new behavior; when she/he wants to accomplish something or to support someone else more than wanting to play it safe; when the person is willing to risk being angry, anxious, caring, driving or retreating, even though these behaviors may make her/him appear foolish or inept or unintelligent or may arouse her/his anxiety. Risk taking may be shown by initiating feedback on one's behavior or by supporting someone when it is not clear what the consequences will be or by giving feedback to others on their behavior.

Your nomination_____ Consensus_____

6. **PROBLEM-CENTERED** when the person focuses on problems facing a group rather than on control or method; when she/he tries to learn by solving problems her/himself rather than by using someone else's solutions. Problem-centering may be seen in one's efforts to find out what is blocking a group, to increase personal effectiveness, and to probe beyond the symptoms. Problem-centering assumes that more work gets done when individuals and groups learn how to solve problems than when they maintain the same pattern of method, control, leadership, or feedback.

Your nomination_____ Consensus_____

Source: From Nominations: Personal Instrumented Feedback in W.J. Pfeiffer and J.E. Jones, (Eds.) (1974). *A handbook for structured experiences in human relations training*, pp. 33-38. Copyright 1974 by Pfeiffer & Co. This material is used by permission of Pfeiffer/Jossey-Bass, Inc., a subsidiary of John Wiley & Sons, Inc.

ACTIVITY 2-13: A Letter to Myself

IN THE CLASSROOM: Writing this letter will help you to focus on your goal(s) for participating in the class. It will also assist in preparing you for the discussion of the syllabus, norms, and goal setting for the class.

IN THE FIELD: *Letter to Myself* is a suitable activity for groups, school age through adult, to promote thoughtful engagement in the group process. Reading and writing skill levels are principal considerations in using the *Letter to Myself.* Adapting the requirements of the activity appropriately to permit maximum participation by group members with various circumstances (age level, physical abilities) is also important in using this activity successfully. Members can write letters by hand, type them as a take-home activity (useful in cases where members use a Braille typewriter or dictate written material using a voice computer program), or dictated to a worker (useful with younger children). For younger children, the letter could be converted to a series of story pictures with a sentence or two about one or two goals. Where promoting shared responsibility is important, ask group members to exchange letters and hold them until the appointed return date. You should discuss how they will keep the letters safe until then.

MATERIALS: Letter forms, envelops, pens

GROUP SIZE: Unlimited

TIME REQUIRED: 15 minutes

SPACE REQUIREMENTS: Sufficient space for students to have private writing space.

PREPARATION: Bring a pen and a self-addressed envelope to the session. The instructor will duplicate the *Letter* forms for the class. Review the *Letter* form below and raise any points for clarification with your instructor.

INSTRUCTIONS: The instructor will distribute the forms. You should be prepared to participate in a discussion of your expectations for the partnership among students and with the instructor, your views on the importance of articulating individual and group goals for the semester's experiences, and ways that you see this exercise providing a basis for developing those goals and norms that will govern the class members' cooperative work in the class. When the discussion is concluded, complete the form in the next ten minutes. When the form is completed, seal it in your envelope. Exchange envelops with a classmate for return at the last class session.

PRACTITIONER'S NOTES:

· With what types of groups would you use this activity?

· At what stage(s) of group development would this activity be useful?

· How would member's characteristics, skills, and abilities influence the way you would modify and implement this activity?

· How would this activity contribute to the group goals, members' goals, and session goals?

· At what point in the group meeting would you introduce the activity?

· How would you evaluate the usefulness and impact of the activity on the group and its members?

A LETTER TO MYSELF

INSTRUCTIONS: On the paper provided, answer the following questions briefly. Seal the letter in the envelope; write your name on the envelope. The instructor will return the letter to you at the last class of the semester.

1. What do you want to accomplish in this course–

   academically,

   socially,

   for personal growth and change?

2. What new things will you try? Name at least three.

3. What is your biggest fear about this new beginning?

4. What will you do to manage this fear?

5. How do you think you will have changed by the end of the semester?

ACTIVITY 2-14: The Reflecting Pool

IN THE CLASSROOM: *The Reflecting Pool* will introduce you to reflective practice. You will begin the process of reflection with an assessment of those skills, abilities, attitudes, and characteristics that you bring to the class.

IN THE FIELD: *The Reflecting Pool* is a suitable activity for older teens and adults. As with classroom groups, you can use this activity in the preaffiliation stage to help members to engage with the group. In the intimacy phase this activity can help to enhance group cohesion by articulating the strengths each member brings to the group. It can assist in deepening the connections among group members and in raising concerns they have about their membership in the group. One set of stones could represent the connections, and the other set could symbolize concerns. At the separation phase you can introduce this activity to assist group members in summing up their individual experiences with the group, their perceptions of the whole group's experiences, and to identify what each will take from the group. At this stage of group development, the first set of stones may represent what members brought to the group and the second would represent what has been gained (or lost) through the group experience.

The combination of water, stones, and a glass or pottery bowl may provide what Fritz Redl (1966) called "gadgetorial seduction," irresistibly inviting splashing and breakage. Thus, the activity may be contraindicated for groups with low impulse control. If you cannot use water in the setting where you would like to do this activity, you could simulate the pool with a mirror and place objects on the mirror. Similarly, a photograph or drawing of a pool and individual objects could substitute for the actual water and stones.

MATERIALS: A large, shallow glass or pottery bowl; an assortment of stones in various sizes, colors, and textures; two baskets to hold the stones; a quantity of water that will fill the bowl almost to the brim once all the stones are placed in the bowl; a container with screw top to transport the water to the site of the session; and a roll of paper towels to mop up spills. If using a table for the activity, placing the bowl on a mat to protect the table from water spotting would be useful.

GROUP SIZE: 15-20

TIME REQUIRED: 15-20 minutes, based on group size.

SPACE REQUIREMENTS: A room or outdoor space, with or without a table and chairs, large enough for the class to form a seated circle around the bowl.

PREPARATION: The instructor will be responsible for selecting a large, attractive shallow bowl, one large stone, and an assortment of smaller stones of various sizes and colors that will give each class member two stones to place in the bowl. Stones that change dramatically when placed under water are especially attractive for this exercise. To check on the amount of water necessary, place all the stones in the bowl, adding enough water to fill the bowl almost to the brim. Remove and dry the stones. Pour the water into the container for transport to the site of the session. At the site the instructor will assemble the materials, placing the two sets of small stones, one set in each basket, and pouring the water into the bowl.

INSTRUCTIONS: In preparing to participate in this activity, recall what you have read or heard about reflective practice and its importance for developing as a professional social worker. The instructor will place the large stone in the center of the bowl and describe the activity in which the group will engage as a metaphor for reflective practice. In turn, each class member will talk about the metaphors they see in the use of water and the shape and composition of the bowl (i.e., glass, pottery). The large stone could represent the class as a whole, including all of the class members' knowledge, skills, experiences, prejudices, biases, strengths, and challenges. It could also represent the body of knowledge and skills you will acquire during the semester. When your turn comes, you will select one stone from each basket to place in the bowl, one to symbolize something positive that you bring to class and one to symbolize an area for growth or a concern you have as the class begins its work together. When all the class members have placed their stones in the bowl and identified what each stone symbolizes, observe the water, its relationship to the bowl and the bowl's contents. Reflect aloud on the metaphors you draw from your observations and your experience doing the activity.

PRACTITIONER'S NOTES:

· At what stage(s) of group development would this activity be useful?

· How would member's characteristics, skills, and abilities influence the way you would modify and implement this activity?

· How would this activity contribute to the group goals, members' goals, and session goals?

· At what point in the group meeting would you introduce the activity?

· How would you evaluate the usefulness and impact of the activity on the group and its members?

Source: Contributed by Nancy Kelly, MSW, Field Coordinator, University of Maine School of Social Work, Orono, ME.

Chapter 3
Interventions in the Middle Stages of Group Development

INTERVENTIONS IN THE MIDDLE STAGES OF GROUP DEVELOPMENT

The activities in this chapter support your work in the middle stages of group development, the *intimacy stage* where the group member becomes more intensely involved with the group and with each other and the ***differentiation stage*** where the group is working most directly on the purpose for which it was formed. Many of the activities in this section can be used at different stages of group development, and those possibilities are noted in section, *In the Field*. As you work through each of these activities, pay close attention to the ways you respond to action-oriented work. The academic setting in which you are immersed expects that you will be proficient in studying texts, writing papers, and participating in class discussion and debate. Each of these activities demands strong abilities with the verbal and written word. Similarly, agency supervisors and staff as well as members of the groups with whom you will work, particularly in adult groups, may expect a verbal intervention style from you. Consider the implications of your reactions to these less verbal, more action-oriented exercises and the possible responses from classmates and colleagues in your field agency as you expand your action-oriented intervention repertoire. As you think about your professional development, you might enjoy reading Whitney Wright's story of her introduction to action-oriented practice in her article, "But I Want to Do a *Real* Group: A Personal Journey from Snubbing to Loving to Theorizing to Demanding Activity-Based Group Work."

The range of activity types in this chapter emphasizes that program activities in social work practice with groups address the whole person, using visual, auditory, and kinesthetic means to help the group and its members achieve program and personal goals. Although you will find that many of these activities have a discussion or "talking" component, the main focus is on other modes of interaction. For example, one activity uses arts and crafts as the primary medium for work (A 3-2 *Collages*). Activities A 3-4, *Messages*, and A 3-5, *Fruit Basket,* involve quiet and active games, respectively. Large movement activities are represented in A 3-3, *Social Barometer*, and A 3-6, *Circle of Birthdays*. Three activities involve visual creativity. A 3-10, *What Do You See*, asks you to look beyond the surface in photographs to speculate on what the photographer's message might be. In A 3-11, *Do You See What I'm Saying*, you will form small task groups, select a theme, and attempt to convey a non-verbal message creatively through a series of photographs mounted in a collage. A 3-13, *Erin Brockovich*, uses video and drama to teach about case and class advocacy skills. The remaining activities employ more traditional methods—role-play, simulations, and pen/paper activities.

Several activities in this chapter originated in practice and have made a successful transfer to the classroom (e.g., A 3-3 *Social Barometer*; A 3-4, *Messages*; A 3-5, *Fruit Basket,* and the two photography activities—A 3-12, and A 3-13). As in the previous sections, uses in the practice setting are emphasized in the *In the Field* component that appears in each activity. As you consider adapting the activities that you have done in the classroom to your practice in the field, re-read the *Note to Students* in the *Introduction* to refresh your thinking about selecting, preparing, and implementing activities with your group(s). You will also benefit from reading two chapters on program activities in Sundel et al. (1985) *Individual Change Through Small Groups (2nd ed.)*. Vinter has written a useful article on the impact of various activities on group member's behavior. Whittaker discusses the specifics about choosing activities for therapeutic groups. Both articles will help prepare you to use activities more thoughtfully and skillfully.

References:

Vinter, R.D. (1985). Program activities: An analysis of their effects on participant behavior. In M. Sundel, P. Glasser, R. Sarri, and R. Vinter (Eds.). *Individual change through small groups (2nd ed.)*. New York: The Free Press.

Whittaker, J.K. (1985). Program activities: Their selection and use in a therapeutic milieu. In M. Sundel, P. Glasser, R. Sarri, and R. Vinter (Eds.). *Individual change through small groups (2nd ed.)*. New York: The Free Press.

Wright, W. (2002). But I want to do a *real* group: A personal journey from snubbing to loving, to theorizing to demanding activity-based group work. In R. Kurland and A. Malekoff (Eds.). *Stories celebrating group work: It's not always easy to sit on your mouth*. New York: The Haworth Social Work Practice Press.

ACTIVITY 3-1: Fill in the Blanks

IN THE CLASSROOM: *Fill in the Blanks* offers you a way to communicate with classmates about experiences you have had and the thoughts/feelings those activities have elicited. This activity is designed to enhance the possibilities for improved communication and cooperation among class members and with the instructor.

IN THE FIELD: In practice with groups you can use sentence completion exercises in the preaffiliation stage to promote interaction. In later phases these exercises may prove useful if the group gets "stuck" and has difficulty interacting. The activity may be done with small groups of six to eight members sharing directly with the whole group or by using dyads or triads with or without a report-back to the whole group, depending on the goal(s) for the session. These exercises give group members a chance to think through their responses, to focus the discussion, to promote sharing in a natural manner, and to help members realize they are not alone in their feelings or experiences. You will want to give some careful consideration to the choice of sentences, tailoring them to the needs of the group and to the phase of group development. If this activity is used to stimulate discussion of "hot topics," the worker should monitor the groups carefully or opt to lead a discussion with the group as a whole to maintain a level of safety for group members. For groups in which members are less verbal, drawing a picture or creating a collage from magazine pictures may be more effective in eliciting participation in this activity. If this approach is chosen, a single focus for the topic and a limit of three questions allows members to complete the activity in the time allotted.

MATERIALS: *Fill in the Blanks* sheets, pens or pencils, writing surfaces (desks, tables).

GROUP SIZE: 30 maximum, divided into small groups of five or six students.

TIME REQUIRED: 30 minutes—five minutes for the introduction and any questions, 15 minutes for the small group discussion; ten minutes for the report back to the larger group.

SPACE REQUIREMENTS: Classroom plus breakout areas with facilities (table, clip or lapboards) for writing.

PREPARATION: Read the instruction for the activity and raise any issues that need clarification.

INSTRUCTIONS: Join a small group. Once your group has moved to the designated meeting area, read the list of incomplete sentences on the *Fill in the Blanks* sheet given below and take a few minutes to reflect on your possible responses. Fill in the blanks with phrases that describe your situation most accurately. When everyone has completed the sheet, compare responses with other group members, noting the similarities and differences among you. The instructor will be available for consultation if the groups need clarification or other assistance. A report back summarizing each group's findings is optional, depending on the purpose of the activity for this session.

PRACTITIONER'S NOTES:

· With what types of groups would you use this activity?

· At what stage(s) of group development would this activity be useful?

· How would member's characteristics, skills, and abilities influence the way you would modify and implement this activity?

· How would this activity contribute to the group goals, members' goals, and session goals?

· At what point in the group meeting would you introduce the activity?

· How would you evaluate the usefulness and impact of the activity on the group and its members?

FILL IN THE BLANKS

Class participation:

The role I usually take in class is....

The thing that makes me most uneasy in class is....

What I appreciate most about an instructor is....

Life issues:

The most difficult issue in school life is....

The greatest challenge my family life presents for me in relation to school is....

The most effective way I manage to cope is....

The best thing about the ways things are now is....

One thing I plan to change is...

Source: From *Group counseling: Strategies and skills, 4th edition,* by E.E. Jacobs, R.L. Masson, R.L. Harvill Copyright 2002. Reprinted with permission of Brooks/Cole, an imprint of the Wadsworth Group, a division of Thomson Learning. Fax (800) 730-2215.

ACTIVITY 3-2: Collages

IN THE CLASSROOM: In making a group collage with other members of the class, you will have an opportunity to experience an alternate mode of communication and to express your ideas, feelings, and experiences through this medium. Participating in and reflecting on this activity will help you understand some of the dynamics of a group in a particular stage of group development.

IN THE FIELD: In your practice with groups you can use "Who Am I" collages in the preaffiliation stage to assist members in getting acquainted. Later, in the intimacy stage, you can use a variation by having group members create Feelings collages to promote interaction, illustrate commonalities, or deal with group difficulties (e.g., if the group gets "stuck" and has difficulty interacting). In the differentiation phase, the author has used a Focus on the Future collage with teen mothers to facilitate a discussion of planning for future goals. The teens selected pictures from various magazines to illustrate where they hoped to be in five years. The discussion included exploration of the needed preparation to accomplish these goals. The group can also work together on one large collage or make individual contributions to a composite group collage; individual or small group collages may be combined into a large display posted on a wall or other suitable location. In this version members place their individual collages on the paper on the wall, fixing the locations as representing their view of their relationship to the group or their place or role in the group.

Depending on members' characteristics and the specific goals of the activity, materials may be varied to add other textures to the collages beyond the torn, folded, curled paper options. Some group members may object to tearing rather than cutting the paper. It is important to remember that the goal of the activity in this case is to use the media as a way to express feeling. The torn paper method provides a more immediate connection with the materials than interposing a tool (scissors) between the individual and the materials. In circumstances where the feelings are less important to the focus of the activity, scissors may replace the torn paper method. Glue sticks may work better for some groups and in some settings limiting the messiness of other types of glue or paste. Whatever the setting, everyone needs to take care not to damage desk or table surfaces with glue or leave debris in the room after the activity. If other groups use the room, the collage(s) should be removed at the end of the session and stored in the worker's office or taken home by group members.

MATERIALS: Glue or paste; construction paper in various colors or poster board; other items suitable for gluing to construction paper or art boards (e.g., magazine pictures, words clipped from magazines, buttons, beads, feathers, leaves, small shells, pebbles and/or other "found" natural materials). Optional: Large sheet of paper to combine collages, tape or other means to attaching the combined collage to the wall.

GROUP SIZE: Up to 10, 20 if using small groups to produce cooperative design

TIME REQUIRED: 15-30 minutes, depending on follow-up discussion

SPACE REQUIREMENTS: Sufficient surfaces (table(s), drawing boards, floor) and wall space to complete and display the project.

PREPARATION: Either the instructor can assemble the materials or request the class to bring in materials for this activity. In either case, the instructor should make a sample collage to determine pitfalls in the activity and find ways to remedy any problems that arise. The instructor should tape a large sheet of paper on the wall for assembling the group collages into a class collage before the activity begins.

INSTRUCTIONS: Once the instructor has discussed the activity with the class and answered any questions that arise, you will join your small group. Group members will begin by choosing the materials and background sheet to form the base for your contribution to the group collage. Using a torn-paper method, you will tear shapes in colors that symbolize your particular views, feelings, or experiences that are chosen as the focus for the activity. Glue the shapes (and other items, if the project includes them) on the background sheet. When the collages are completed, each group will describe what their collages symbolize and a discussion based on these comments will follow. Reconvene in the classroom and post your group collage on the space provided. Share the meaning of the group's collage with the class when your turn comes.

PRACTITIONER'S NOTES:

· With what types of groups would you use this activity?

· At what stage(s) of group development would this activity be useful?

· How would member's characteristics, skills, and abilities influence the way you would modify and implement this activity?

· How would this activity contribute to the group goals, members' goals, and session goals?

· At what point in the group meeting would you introduce the activity?

· How would you evaluate the usefulness and impact of the activity on the group and its members?

Acknowledgement: The feelings collage is based on discussion in a group work class at Loyola University, Chicago, Elaine Finnegan, Instructor.

ACTIVITY 3-3: Social Barometer

IN THE CLASSROOM: By participating in the *Social Barometer* as a discussion starter activity you will take a stand literally on issues related to the topic for the class session and will see where others in the class stand in relation to your position.

IN THE FIELD: You can use the *Social Barometer* in a variety of settings and with a range of age groups. The *Social Barometer* is suitable for use with groups as small as six to eight or with large workshop groups of 40 to 100. For example, Kay Goler Levin, the contributor of this activity, has used it in an elementary school to talk about sex and birth control. If you are responsible for a staff in-service training you could use it to stimulate discussion of "hot topics" such as race relations, welfare reform, and an assortment of gender issues. In each setting it fosters group discussion and encourages consideration and correction of misconceptions. Placing the numbered papers on the floor before the group starts conversation and speculation about them.

In the preaffiliation stage you can use this activity as an icebreaker. It can foster much physical activity if the instructor consciously alternates statements so that group members move from one extreme to the other. The movement encourages interaction among group members. In the intimacy phase the Social Barometer enhances group cohesion as group members learn who shares some of their opinions. In any applications if some group members have mobility constraints, the activity is adaptable. For example, in an in-service training that Levin conducted, a participant with visual impairment moved with a friend who shared his views. In groups where members use wheelchairs or walkers, the group worker would allow additional time for participants to locate themselves behind numbers. The statements could be signed or posted on an overhead projector in groups where members have hearing impairments.

MATERIALS: List of statements relevant to the discussion topic written on a single sheet of paper or on a series of 3"x5" cards. Barometer marked out on five pieces of paper or poster board large enough for everyone in the room to see them (8 Ω x 11 inches or larger) and taped to the floor. Points on the barometer should read +50, +100, 0, -50, -100, written using brightly colored markers in figures large enough for the whole group to see them on the floor. If the activity takes place outside, the papers need to be tacked down or the numbers written in chalk on cement.

GROUP SIZE: 6-100

TIME REQUIRED: 15-45 minutes, depending on group size, the number of statements for students' reactions, and the amount of interaction the activity engenders.

SPACE REQUIREMENTS: A classroom large enough to accommodate students as a moveable grid on the barometer. Students need to move freely around the room and place themselves on the numbers that best express the way they feel about the statements the instructor makes. If the activity takes place inside, move the chairs to the back of the room, creating an open space in the front.

PREPARATION: Well before the session, the instructor will prepare a series of statements that will help assess where the class members stand on key aspects of the issue(s) to be considered. The statements should be written in positive rather than negative (or double negative) terms. Positive statements are easier to decipher. The instructor will also make the signs for the barometer. The signs can be reused for other topics if they are made from sturdy card stock or poster board.

You may be asked to help the instructor to clear the chairs to the back of the room if the activity is planned for inside. The instructor will place the signs far enough apart so class members can stand behind them comfortably, at least three to five feet apart.

-100	-50	0	+50	+100

INSTRUCTIONS: Listen carefully as the instructor introduces the activity and the focus of the issues on which you will "take a stand." As you participate in the activity, you and your classmates will become a movable grid as you place yourselves behind the number that best expresses your opinions, ideas, and reactions to the statements the instructor reads.

The instructor will begin the activity by reading a simple statement as an example (e.g. Spinach is a tasty vegetable), and invite the class members to stand behind the number that reflects your individual stance on the statement. If you have no opinion or don't know anything about the statement, stand behind 0. Those who agree moderately go to +50. Those who totally agree go to +100. Those who disagree moderately stand behind –50, and those who totally disagree stand behind –100. You and your classmates, thus, become the barometer. The instructor will check with the class to see if you are located behind a number that most reflects your stance on the statement, respond to questions, and clarify any unclear instructions. This is the time for you to make sure you understand what you will be doing in this activity.

Once all the questions have been asked, the instructor will proceed with the actual questions, tallying the responses next to the statements on the written list or cards for later discussion. When the instructor has read all the questions and tallied the responses, you will be seated in a circle and participate in a discussion of the topic based on the responses the class has made in the course of the activity.

PRACTITIONER'S NOTES:

· 	With what types of groups would you use this activity?

· 	At what stage(s) of group development would this activity be useful?

· 	How would member's characteristics, skills, and abilities influence the way you would modify and implement this activity?

· 	How would this activity contribute to the group goals, members' goals, and session goals?

·   At what point in the group meeting would you introduce the activity?

·   How would you evaluate the usefulness and impact of the activity on the group and its members?

Source: Contributed by Kay Goler Levin, ACSW, LCSW, PhD Candidate, Loyola University, Chicago.

ACTIVITY 3-4: Messages

IN THE CLASSROOM: As you participate in the *Messages* activity, you will perceive the importance of a range of communication skills and will experience the ways that messages may become distorted.

IN THE FIELD: *Messages* can be used with groups from children through adults as an energizer, as a way to illustrate issues in communication, or as a light-hearted, non-threatening way to begin dealing with the groups problems in communication. You can vary the activity by repeating the message under different conditions to illustrate aspects of verbal communication that can cause difficulties in the group. One approach is to vary the length of the message to compare the results for short and long messages. Then you can facilitate a discussion of possible comparisons. For example, note that complicated messages tend to change as they move from individual to individual. Receivers may reduce the message to a manageable form, sharpening the high points and forgetting the rest. Varying the level of vocabulary by using less familiar or more technical terms illustrates the tendency for the receivers to assimilate the message by filtering it through their own frames of reference. Follow up with a discussion of the barriers to communication illustrated by the variations of the activity.

To illustrate the importance of checking for accuracy, complete the activity a second time with a different message. Alter the rules to allow the receiver to clarify the message. Complete the activity and discuss the results. Note that checking back tends to increase the accuracy of the reception, reduces distortion and incompleteness of the message. Follow up with a discussion of ways to enhance communication.

You can change the conditions for sending the message to decrease or increase the difficulty of the process. For example, you can ask the group members to be silent except when delivering the message. Reducing the background noise tends to decrease the difficulty in hearing the message. Allowing the group to chat while they wait their turn amplifies the noise level in the room and tends to increase the difficulty in hearing the message accurately. Ask the group to consider external barriers to communication and ways to improve good communication by adjusting environmental conditions. If you are working with a group whose principal way of communicating is through signing, you can ask all but the two persons sending and receiving the message to close their eyes. To alert the next participant, the new sender taps the next receiver lightly on the shoulder.

MATERIALS: None

GROUP SIZE: 4 to unlimited

TIME REQUIRED: 5 minutes minimum, depending on class size.

SPACE REQUIREMENTS: Sufficient room to form a circle with enough space between students to eliminate the possibility of overhearing the message.

PREPARATION: The instructor will locate two quotations or create sentence(s) relevant to the group situation. One should be fairly long and unfamiliar; the second should be short and familiar.

Sample Message – long and unfamiliar: Freud said, "He that has eyes to see and ears to hear may convince himself that no mortal can keep a secret. While his lips are silent, he chatters with his fingertips; betrayal oozes out of him at every pore". (www.brainyquote.com)

Sample Message – short and familiar: Jack and Jill went up the hill to fetch a pail of water.

INSTRUCTIONS: The instructor will whisper the message to the first student as clearly as possible at a normal rate of speech, but only once. The receiver will whisper the message to the person next to her or him. The message is whispered from person to person until everyone has received and re-sent the message. The last person to receive the message repeats it aloud to the group. When the class has completed delivery of the message to the last person, the instructor will facilitate a discussion of the various influences you think had a bearing on the success or failure of getting the message through to the last person. You will also consider the implications for practice.

PRACTITIONER'S NOTES:

·   At what stage(s) of group development would this activity be useful?

·   How would member's characteristics, skills, and abilities influence the way you would modify and implement this activity?

·   How would this activity contribute to the group goals, members' goals, and session goals?

·   At what point in the group meeting would you introduce the activity?

·   How would you evaluate the usefulness and impact of the activity on the group and its members?

ACTIVITY 3-5: Fruit Basket

IN THE CLASSROOM: In *Fruit Basket* you will gain some practice with listening skills.

IN THE FIELD: *Fruit Basket* is suitable for groups of school-age children and teens in circumstances where the participants do not have mobility restrictions. It can be used as an icebreaker early in the group's development and as an energizer in later stages of group development. Because of its focus on listening and communicating clearly, it is a low-key way of approaching issues in communication. The focus of the story can vary depending on the group's circumstances. This game is unsuitable for members with mobility restrictions. Its rowdiness potential is high. The group worker needs to be alert in stopping the game before that level is reached. Lightweight chairs that tip easily should be avoided.

MATERIALS: A circle of sturdy, armless chairs, one per student.

GROUP SIZE: 30 maximum.

TIME REQUIRED: 10 minutes.

SPACE REQUIREMENTS: An indoor or outdoor space large enough to create a large circle.

PREPARATION: Arrange the chairs in a large circle.

INSTRUCTIONS: You will take a seat in the circle. Listen carefully as the instructor tells the class the procedures for doing the activity. *Fruit Basket* is a storytelling game about creating a fruit salad. You will use your listening skills as the storyteller relates how to create the fruit salad and you will or will not respond to the verbal cues to the story as it unfolds depending on how well you are listening. You will be assigned one of four fruit categories—apples, oranges, bananas, pineapples—and you will need to be alert for your category if or when it is mentioned in the story. When you hear your category mentioned, you will change seats quickly with other members of that category. If, as the story unfolds, you hear the words, Fruit Basket, everyone changes seats. Whenever some or all of the participants change seats, the storyteller tries to get a seat in the circle. The goal of the game is always to have a seat in the circle. The person left without a seat becomes the next storyteller.

The instructor will select the first storyteller either by asking for a volunteer or assigning someone the role. The storyteller's seat will be removed from the circle. The game will proceed until five or six participants have been the storyteller. When the game is over, you will debrief the activity by discussing your observations and experiences as listeners and storytellers. Consider the connections to what you know about listening skills and what might interfere with using effective listening.

PRACTITIONER'S NOTES:

- At what stage(s) of group development would this activity be useful?

- How would member's characteristics, skills, and abilities influence the way you would modify and implement this activity?

·   How would this activity contribute to the group goals, members' goals, and session goals?

·   At what point in the group meeting would you introduce the activity?

·   How would you evaluate the usefulness and impact of the activity on the group and its members?

Source: Youth groups where the author was a member.

ACTIVITY 3-6: Circle of Birthdays

IN THE CLASSROOM: In the *Circle of Birthdays* you will experience an alternate form of communication in a quick and simple exercise.

IN THE FIELD: You might use *Circle of Birthdays* at two different stages of group development. In the preaffiliation stage of group development it can serve as an icebreaker. In the intimacy stage you might use it as an energizer and an additional way for members to connect with each other. Beyond demonstrating an alternate mode of communication, the exercise may be used to sort people into small groups for other activities using seasons of the year where the birthdays occur. In any case, remind the group that the focus of the activity is on the month and day of birth, not the year, thus avoiding issues around age.

MATERIALS: None

GROUP SIZE: 30 maximum

TIME REQUIRED: 15 minutes

SPACE REQUIREMENTS: Enough floor space to accommodate all the students in a circle

PREPARATION: The instructor will ask you to help clear enough space in the room to allow space to form a circle including all the class members.

INSTRUCTIONS: The class members will form a circle. Without speaking, you will rearrange their position in the circle to reflect the month in which they were born. Within the month groupings, students will arrange their position in the circle by the day of the month on which they were born. The circle should begin with those having January birthdays and continue through to the end with those having December birthdays. To discover your proper place in the circle, you will need to find ways to communicate your birth date and compare it to those next to you. When the class is satisfied that everyone is in the right spot, the instructor will ask the person with the earliest birth date to state the month and date to the class. The remaining members will state their birth dates in order. The class will be seated and participate in a short reflection on what you each have experienced in this activity and the implications you find for your practice.

PRACTITIONER'S NOTES:

· At what stage(s) of group development would this activity be useful?

· How would member's characteristics, skills, and abilities influence the way you would modify and implement this activity?

· How would this activity contribute to the group goals, members' goals, and session goals?

·   At what point in the group meeting would you introduce the activity?

·   How would you evaluate the usefulness and impact of the activity on the group and its members?

Source: Contributed by Marcia B. Cohen, PhD, Professor, University of New England School of Social Work, Portland, ME.

ACTIVITY 3-7: Empathic Responses

IN THE CLASSROOM: In *Empathic Responses* you will focus your attention on empathic modes of recognizing and communicating about feelings and emotions, and you will gain practice in using empathic communication.

IN THE FIELD: You can use both the Feelings Vocabulary and an accompanying Role-play with treatment or in-service training groups in situations where you want to encourage group members to consider the ways they interact currently and the ways that change in those behaviors might improve the life of the group. You can vary the words selected for the Feelings Vocabulary lists and the choice of Role-play to reinforce the concepts you wish to emphasize with the group.

MATERIALS: Activity sheets, pencils, paper for taking notes on the role-play.

GROUP SIZE: 30

TIME REQUIRED: 30-45 minutes, depending on group size, the initial question period, and the debriefing discussion following the activity.

SPACE REQUIREMENTS: Classroom plus small breakout spaces for task groups to conduct the Role-play with as little noise interference as possible.

PREPARATION: The instructor will arrange the room to support the activity.

INSTRUCTIONS: Read the activity sheet, and raise any questions you may have about the instructions. When the class has divided into the task groups, each of you will complete the Feelings Vocabulary sheet independently. Then your task group will complete the role-play and hold a short discussion based on the observers' notes and the player's responses. The instructor will be available for consultation if the groups have further questions or need clarification. When the task groups have completed the role-play, you will reconvene as a class and debrief the activity. The discussion will focus on responses to each of the two exercises and lessons learned from the role-play experience.

PRACTITIONER'S NOTES:

·   At what stage(s) of group development would this activity be useful?

·   How would member's characteristics, skills, and abilities influence the way you would modify and implement this activity?

·   How would this activity contribute to the group goals, members' goals, and session goals?

·   At what point in the group meeting would you introduce the activity?

·   How would you evaluate the usefulness and impact of the activity on the group and its members?

PART A: DEVELOPING A FEELINGS VOCABULARY [5 Minutes]

Responding to feelings expressed by clients and to the underlying feeling tone necessitates developing an extensive vocabulary of words to denote feeling states. Using the categories listed below and without consulting other group members, you will list 5 words, which convey some aspect of each category. You should have 30 words when finished.

FEELINGS VOCABULARY

Happiness   Hurt and loss   Anxiety and fear   Sadness   Anger   Guilt

1.

2.

3.

4.

5.

Source: From *The social work skills workbook, 1ˢᵗ edition*, by B. Cournoyer. Copyright 1991. Reprinted with permission of Brooks/Cole, an imprint of the Wadsworth Group, a division of Thomson Learning. Fax 800 730-2215.

PART B: ROLE-PLAY [10 Minutes]

THE TASK: Now that you have considered the Feelings Vocabulary, you will practice using this vocabulary in the following role-play situation. The group should decide who will play each role. The remaining group members will act as observers to write down each feeling expressed by the client and the worker's empathic response. These responses can be of two types: a. reflecting the feeling(s) expressed by the client; b. using additive empathy (i.e., going beyond what is said to help the client explore the underlying feelings which may be implied by the client's words, tone, body language).

THE ROLES:

1. The worker: a staff member at the local family and children's counseling center. The worker has worked for this agency for six months and earned a BSW earlier this year.

2. The client: Mrs. Hernandez, who has recently moved to Bangor, Maine when her husband was transferred by his company. She is originally from Mexico and attempts to preserve her heritage by insuring that her two children speak Spanish as well as English. The children attend a local grade school. Blanca is eight and Jorge is ten.

THE SITUATION: Mrs. Hernandez is looking for some assistance in dealing with the local school. Specifically, she is worried about the safety of her children because they have been called names and shoved around at school and on the way home by four older white children who live in the Hernandez's neighborhood. As she and the worker discuss the situation, Mrs. H. relates how upset she is and how impossible it is to talk with the teachers and the guidance counselor. She feels she has to fight very hard for a hearing and for the school's recognition of the unsafe conditions her children experience there. She also reports that fighting what she interprets as racist attitudes is exhausting and that perhaps she should just accept things as they are. After all, she is only one woman against the system in an area that is nearly 100% white in a state where you rarely see a person of color or one whose first language is Spanish.

THE FOLLOW UP DISCUSSION: [10 minutes] The observers will compare notes and report their observations to the worker. The worker and the client will address the level of accuracy of the observations as compared with the feelings they were attempting to convey during the interview.

THE DEBRIEFING: [5minutes] The class will reconvene. The instructor will lead a discussion of the responses to the activity, asking the group to note their experiences developing a feelings vocabulary and their initial learning from.

Source: From *The social work skills workbook*, 1st edition, by B. Cournoyer. Copyright 1991. Adapted with permission of Brooks/Cole, an imprint of the Wadsworth Group, a division of Thomson Learning. Fax 800 730-2215.

ACTIVITY 3-8: Observation and Listening Skills

IN THE CLASSROOM: This activity will provide you with an opportunity to practice active listening and focused observation in gathering information of assessment using an eco-map. You will also gain some practice in giving and receiving constructive criticism.

IN THE FIELD: This activity is suitable primarily for use in agency-based staff training. Using the Practitioner's Notes, consider ways you might adapt it for use with other types of groups in the practice setting.

MATERIALS: Readings on communication skills [e.g., Chapter Two: Micro Practice Skills: Working with Individuals. In K.K. Kirst-Ashman, & G.H. Hull, Jr. (2002). *Understanding generalist practice (3rd ed.)*. Pacific Grove, CA: Brooks/Cole; Chapter 8: Basic Communication and Helping Skills. In B.W. Schaefor, C.R. Horesji & G.A. Horesji (1997). *Techniques and guidelines for social work practice*], a copy of the instruction sheet and role-play.

GROUP SIZE: 30-40

TIME REQUIRED: 60 minutes.

SPACE REQUIREMENTS: Classroom with breakout areas where task groups can conduct individual role-plays with as little interference from the surroundings as possible.

PREPARATION: Prior to the activity, you should complete the assigned reading and participate in a class discussion of the skills to be used: active listening, observation, collecting data for developing an eco-map.

INSTRUCTIONS: Read the instructions for the activity and the role-play below and raise questions and points needing clarification. The class will divide into task groups of four to six members. The objective for your small group is to complete the role-play and discussion outlined below. You will have 45 minutes to complete the activity and should be aware of the time constraints. The instructor will check in with the groups once early in the activity to answer questions or clarify any difficulties that may have arisen and will be available for consultation as needed. When the class reconvenes, you should be prepared to discuss your reactions to the activity, emphasizing your perceptions of professional use of active listening and observation skills.

PRACTITIONER'S NOTES:

·   At what stage(s) of group development would this activity be useful?

·   How would member's characteristics, skills, and abilities influence the way you would modify and implement this activity?

·   How would this activity contribute to the group goals, members' goals, and session goals?

· At what point in the group meeting would you introduce the activity?

· How would you evaluate the usefulness and impact of the activity on the group and its members?

Role-play: Observation and Listening Skills

INSTRUCTIONS: In the next 45 minutes your task group will complete the following items:

1. **Roles:** Using the *Situation* below, determine who will fulfill the following roles: client, social worker, observer(s), social worker's consultant. The consultant will be available to the worker if the worker gets "stuck" or wishes other guidance during "time outs" in the interview process. Review the role-play situation and assume roles.

2. **Role-Play:** The worker and the client will role-play the situation until the worker has elicited sufficient information to develop a useful eco-map for initial assessment. Be aware of the time limits for the activity.

3. *Discussion:* As a task group, discuss what the worker did with respect to active listening and focused observation. Consider how effective the worker's listening and observation skills were in relation to the task assigned. Seek feedback first from the client, then self-evaluation from the worker, then comments from the observer(s) and consultant. Comments should be concrete, phrased positively wherever possible, and offer specific guidance for improving listening and observation skills. As observer(s) and consultant, consider what facilitated your listening/observation skills and enabled you to provide useful feedback to the worker.

SITUATION:

Mrs. Davis is an employed mother with three children (Joanna, 7; Mark, 2 1/2; Trina, 6 months). She has been seeing a social worker at a local community center on an individual basis for three sessions. In the previous session she complained that her mother, Mrs. Thomas, who cares for the children during the day, is undermining her authority with the youngsters. As a result, Mrs. Davis feels that they are becoming unmanageable. Many arguments between Mr. and Mrs. Davis revolve around the children's behavior. Mrs. Davis feels that she has no other alternative for day care given the high cost of home day care for the infant and toddler and the relative unavailability of after-school care for the seven-year-old. Her company is not one of the few in the area that provide on-site day care or day care vouchers for employees. Mrs. Davis reports that Mrs. Thomas disapproves of casework services and feels that a mother's place is with her children, especially when they are very young.

ACTIVITY 3-9: Verbal Intervention Skills

IN THE CLASSROOM: In this activity you will practice verbal interventions focusing on affect, cognition, and behavior in a simulated interview. You will have an opportunity to increase your experience in giving and receiving constructive criticism with classmates in a simulated peer supervision group.

IN THE FIELD: Role-plays focusing on skill development are appropriate for use in staff group supervision, agency in-service training, and professional development workshops. Using the Practitioner's Notes as a guide, consider ways you might adapt this activity for use in groups in your field or practice setting.

MATERIALS: Readings on verbal interventions [e.g., Chapter Two: Micro Practice Skills: Working with Individuals. In K.K. Kirst-Ashman, & G.H. Hull, Jr. (2002). *Understanding generalist practice (3rd ed.)*. Pacific Grove, CA: Brooks/Cole; Chapter 8: Basic Communication and Helping Skills. In B.W. Schaefor, C.R. Horesji & G.A. Horesji (1997). *Techniques and guidelines for social work practice*], a copy of the role-play instructions.

GROUP SIZE: 30-40

TIME REQUIRED: 45-50 minutes

SPACE REQUIREMENTS: Classroom with smaller breakout areas for task groups.

PREPARATION: Before engaging in this activity, you should have completed the readings on verbal interventions. Also read the role-play instructions. Take this opportunity to raise questions and areas that may need further discussion.

INSTRUCTIONS: On the day of the activity, raise any additional questions that you may have based on the readings and/or the role-play instructions. Next, the class will divide into smaller task groups. Each group will take the first five minutes of their small group meeting to select roles as the worker, client, or observer. The worker and client will role-play the second session as outlined in the instructions. The role-play should last no more than 15 minutes. As the worker and client role-play the second session, the observer will chart the interaction using the checklist of verbal responses in the instructions. The observer will note the number of times the worker uses each of the various procedures. The remaining group members will identify and track the focus of the worker's strategy to discern whether the worker is targeting the intervention plan primarily to affect, cognition, or behavior. Group members should be prepared to support their choice with specific examples from the interaction between the worker and client. The instructor will be available for consultation at any point during the activity.

After the role-play is completed, the task groups will take the next 10 minutes to discuss the results of the observation. About five minutes before the activity is scheduled to end, the instructor will check with each group to make sure that you will complete the activity on time. Reconvene as a class and participate in debriefing the activity. You will focus on verbal interventions most/least frequently used and intervention strategies most/least frequently used. Speculate on the reasons and the consequences of the choices made for the conduct of the case.

PRACTITIONER'S NOTES:

· At what stage(s) of group development would this activity be useful?

· How would member's characteristics, skills, and abilities influence the way you would modify and implement this activity?

· How would this activity contribute to the group goals, members' goals, and session goals?

· At what point in the group meeting would you introduce the activity?

· How would you evaluate the usefulness and impact of the activity on the group and its members?

VERBAL INTERVENTIONS ROLE-PLAY

INSTRUCTIONS: Before class, read the attached Role-play situation. In the task group, select a triad consisting of the worker, client, observer. The worker and client will role-play the second session. The role-play should last no more than 15 minutes. Use the attached checklists to guide your observations and take notes.

Observer's tasks: Observe the interaction between the worker and the client. Note on the form given below the number of times the worker uses the various verbal interventions.

Group members' tasks:

1. Identify the focus of the worker's strategy. Is the worker targeting the intervention primarily to affect, cognition, or behavior? Support your choice with specific points in the interaction between the worker and client. In groups where there are only three members, add the group member's tasks to the observer's tasks.

2. Discuss the results of the observation with the observer reporting the tally of verbal interventions and allowing for reaction and response from the worker. Then discuss the group members' views of the primary focus of the session. Speculate with the worker on the suitability and usefulness of the approach and what might be the impact on the future work with the client. [Item # 2 should take no more than 15 min.]

3. Rejoin the class and be prepared to report on the results of the observations.

ROLE-PLAY SITUATION

Background Information: Celia Jones is a 27-year-old woman. She is married to Ronald Jones, has one 3-year-old child, Lucy, and works part-time at a local factory. She has sought counseling from this family service agency at the suggestion of the social worker at Lucy's day care center. The reason for the referral was that both Ms. Jones and the social worker feel that the parents need help with parenting skills, especially in the area of discipline. Lucy is very active, has a short attention span, and is difficult to discipline. When at home, she spends the most time in the family's three-room apartment, which is on the third floor of the six-flat where they live in town. Ms. Jones is reluctant to let her child play outside with the other children in the fenced-in yard and has little energy to go to the park. Discipline at home is very uneven, depending on how tired Ms. Jones is and how irritated Mr. Jones is when he gets home from work.

Session Two: Ms. Jones has been seen twice at the agency, once for intake and once for the first session in which she gave the worker the information listed above and agreed to keep a behavior log. She would use the log to record times when Lucy's behavior became difficult and one of the parents administered discipline. During this session the worker will check with Ms. Jones about the behavior log she has been keeping so that they can develop a baseline for the parent-child interaction.

VERBAL INTERVENTIONS

INSTRUCTIONS: Review the definitions of verbal interventions typically used in social work practice. Use the list as a guide in observing the interactions between the worker and the client in the role-play.

Acceptance: an understanding attitude that does not necessarily approve of the client's thoughts, feelings, attitudes, and/or actions.

Encouragement: worker responses that support and urge the client to continue the discussion.

Reassurance: reality-based comments regarding the client's situation; usually used infrequently.

Advice-giving: suggestions for courses of action; usually used sparingly.

Exploration: describing the facts from either the client's or the worker's perspective.

Rephrasing: restating what the client has said in different words; used to clarify whether worker has heard the client accurately and to demonstrate attentive listening.

Clarification: making sure that the worker understands the full intent of the client's words clearly and accurately.

Reflection: drawing out what the worker surmises that the client may be feeling about the circumstances the client has described.

Summarizing: drawing the session or a segment of the session to a close with a brief review of the key points previously discussed.

OBSERVER'S CHECKLIST

INSTRUCTIONS: Record the number of times the worker uses the verbal interventions listed below.

ACCEPTANCE:

ENCOURAGEMENT:

REASSURANCE:

ADVICE-GIVING:

EXPLORATION:

REPHRASING:

CLARIFICATION;

REFLECTION:

SUMMARIZING:

TARGETS OF WORKER ACTIVITY

AFFECT: The worker's principal focus is on the client system's affect or feelings relating to the topic under discussion. The worker notes and responds to feelings expressed in the session and those linked to situation that has brought the client to seek help.

COGNITION: The worker's main focus is on the client system's thoughts on the subject discussed. The client system's thought patterns, intellectual capabilities, and formal/informal educational experience help shape the style and direction of the worker's approach.

BEHAVIOR: The worker's primary focus is on the client system's actions and performance in the situation being considered. The worker also notes the client system's conduct during the session. The worker considers discrepancies between affect, cognition, and behavior as they are present either in the session or in the client system's self report.

GROUP MEMBER'S CHECKLIST

INSTRUCTIONS: Select the principal target of the worker's activity using the definitions below.

WORKER ACTIVITIES TARGETED TO -

AFFECT:

COGNITION:

BEHAVIOR:

PRINCIPAL FOCUS:

ACTIVITY 3-10: What Do You See?

IN THE CLASSROOM: In *What Do You See?* you will explore the similarities and differences in perception of the situations depicted in the photos chosen. This activity will introduce another mode of communication that you can use in your practice with groups.

IN THE FIELD: You can use photography-based activities with a wide range of populations as a non-threatening discussion starter for various topics. If it is impractical to post the photos, using slides and a slide projector or photos scanned in for a Power Point presentation would also work well. You might also consider using picture books with some groups. For example, Walter Wick has produced a series of *I Spy* books of picture riddles. Group members hunt for a variety of objects secreted in the pictures. *I Spy Treasure Hunt: A Book of Picture Riddles* is one in the series that is well suited to use as an alternative for this activity or as a fun way to introduce the series of photo activities. Using the *Practitioner's Notes*, consider the range of applications this type of activity might have in your field placement.

MATERIALS: Large photos from a photography club on campus or elsewhere or copied from art photography books, masking tape, a small notepad and pencil.

GROUP SIZE: 30 maximum

TIME REQUIRED: 30 minutes minimum.

SPACE REQUIREMENTS: A classroom that accommodates students walking around to view the photos; seating from which to view the photos comfortably and have a class discussion.

PREPARATION: The instructor will select a short series of photos that support the focus of the topic for the group activity, given the group composition, stage of group development, and the topic and purpose of the session. Based on the topic and purpose of the session, the instructor will devise a suggested list of things to observe in the photos. Before the session begins, the instructor will post the photos around the room at a height allowing the class to view them easily while standing or seated.

INSTRUCTIONS: The class will divide into teams of three to five students. Using the notepads and pencils, you will move around the room to view the photos and make notes of your observations. You will have 10 minutes to view the photos and make notes. Each team will meet for 10 minutes to organize their collected observations for the discussion. When the class reconvenes, each small group will report its observations as a way to begin discussion of the session topic.

PRACTITIONER'S NOTES:

·   At what stage(s) of group development would this activity be useful?

·   How would member's characteristics, skills, and abilities influence the way you would modify and implement this activity?

·   How would this activity contribute to the group goals, members' goals, and session goals?

·   At what point in the group meeting would you introduce the activity?

·   How would you evaluate the usefulness and impact of the activity on the group and its members?

Additional resource: Wick, W. & Marzollo, J. (1999). *I spy treasure hunt: A book of picture riddles.* New York: Scholastic Books, Inc.

Source: From a private communication with David Parsons, Photographer, Lynn, MA. Adapted with permission.

ACTIVITY 3-11: Do You See What I'm Saying?

IN THE CLASSROOM: In *Do You See What I'm Saying?* you will work on developing alternative methods for communicating thoughts, information, and feelings on a particular theme relevant to the group and its members.

IN THE FIELD: You can use this activity in groups supporting normal growth and development (e.g., after-school and recreational programs) to focus on themes connected with the purposes of those groups and the interests of members. In therapeutic groups, you might have group members use photography to express thoughts, feelings, and issues difficult to verbalize as another avenue for communication. Be aware that cost may be a problematic element in this activity. Explore the possibility of donations of equipment and photographic supplies from a local camera club or of soliciting a local merchant to donate disposable cameras. If disposable cameras are used, they should be the indoor/outdoor variety so that groups will not be limited in the locations where they will take photographs.

MATERIALS: You will be responsible for providing the equipment for this project, including: one camera per group (disposable cameras will work as long as you purchase a model for indoor and outdoor photography), film—36 exposures, photo processing outlet; poster board; art supplies for completing poster.

GROUP SIZE: 30

TIME REQUIRED: Students' preparation time outside class: one day to take the photographs; time for developing the prints (varies depending on available photo processing outlets); time to prepare photo poster presentation. In class time: one hour total—30 minutes for two class sessions.

SPACE REQUIREMENTS: Wall space to accommodate posters.

PREPARATION: The instructor will prepare and duplicate the instruction sheet early in the semester, giving your groups sufficient time to prepare, implement, and complete the activity.

INSTRUCTIONS:

Two sessions before the posters will be presented: The instructor will introduce the activity by asking you to list all the ways that people communicate with each other. When the class has exhausted all the possibilities, you will divide into small task groups. Review the instruction sheet independently, noting that your group will select a theme from the list provided and plan the types of photographs that will convey something significant about the theme. You will each select an aspect of the theme and be responsible for taking a series of photos to illustrate that aspect. You will be responsible for having the photos developed in time for the group to complete the poster.

Poster Session: The class members will arrange the wall and/or table space in the classroom to accommodate the posters and set up the posters. When the posters are in place, you will have 10 minutes to view them. Then the class will be seated. Each group will present their commentary on the theme of their poster and discuss briefly the key points in the group's process in completing the activity and the major lesson(s) learned from the experience. As a class, you will decide where the posters will be displayed, if the group agrees on sharing their work with the larger university community.

PRACTITIONER'S NOTES:

·   At what stage(s) of group development would this activity be useful?

·   How would member's characteristics, skills, and abilities influence the way you would modify and implement this activity?

·   How would this activity contribute to the group goals, members' goals, and session goals?

·   At what point in the group meeting would you introduce the activity?

·   How would you evaluate the usefulness and impact of the activity on the group and its members?

Source: From a private communication with David Parsons, Photographer, Lynn, MA. Adapted with permission.

DO YOU SEE WHAT I'M SAYING?

INSTRUCTIONS: The goal of this project is to create a poster that will convey a significant aspect of the theme selected by the group. The group should complete the following steps in creating the poster:

1. Select a theme from the list provided.

2. Plan the types of photographs that will convey something significant about the theme.

3. Schedule a time when all group members can participate in the photo shoot.

4. Assemble the needed equipment—camera, film, art supplies.

5. Shoot the entire roll of film. (Written permission is needed if you photograph individuals.)

6. Have the film developed.

7. Select a series of photos for the poster.

8. Design the poster.

9. Prepare a brief, written commentary on the theme, key points in the group's process in completing the activity, and major lesson(s) learned from the experience.

POSSIBLE THEMES:

- Seasons of life

- Daily work

- Poverty

- Having fun

- Communication

- Gender roles

- Childhood

- Aging

- Care-giving

- Other ideas [Please obtain prior approval from the instructor.]

ACTIVITY 3-12: Homeless in Bangor: Implementing a Community-Based Task Group

IN THE CLASSROOM: In this activity you will explore the use of community-based task groups in addressing a community problem.

IN THE FIELD: If you are responsible for staff training in work with community groups, you can adapt this activity for training purposes. This activity will give staff an opportunity to explore the issues involved in working in community coalitions and to improve skills in working with broadly conceived task groups. Using the Practitioner's Notes as a guide, consider ways you might adapt this activity for your practice.

MATERIALS: Chairs, tables or other available writing space, flip chart sheets, large markers, masking tape.

GROUP SIZE: 30

TIME REQUIRED: 45 minutes, minimum.

SPACE REQUIREMENTS: Classroom plus smaller areas for breakout groups.

PREPARATION: Read the instruction sheet in the class before the activity will be used and raise questions or points for clarification. In the next class session bring your notes on recommendations for the two main tasks in this activity: recommending additional task force members and addressing the list of goals for the community coalition.

INSTRUCTIONS: Divide into task groups of five or six members each. Select a large marker and two sheets of flip chart paper. The groups will meet for one-half hour. Select a recorder who will list the group's responses to the two tasks and deliver the report to the class. When the class reconvenes, report your recommendations for the composition of the community coalition, the goals, and the rationale for your choices. The instructor will facilitate a discussion and evaluation of each group's proposals.

PRACTITIONER'S NOTES:

- At what stage(s) of group development would this activity be useful?

- How would member's characteristics, skills, and abilities influence the way you would modify and implement this activity?

- How would this activity contribute to the group goals, members' goals, and session goals?

- At what point in the group meeting would you introduce the activity?

· How would you evaluate the usefulness and impact of the activity on the group and its members?

Source: From Alexander, G. (1996). Project homeless. In R.F. Rivas & G.H. Hull, Jr. *Case studies in generalist practice*. Pacific Grove, CA: Brooks/Cole Publishing Co., p. 133. Adapted with permission from the author.

HOMELESS IN BANGOR: A COMMUNITY/UNIVERSITY PARTNERSHIP

The Problem: Homelessness takes many forms in Bangor. Some homeless people (e.g., teens, people with mental illness) are quite visible on downtown streets; others are largely invisible. They are often whole families who double up with friends or relatives, sharing their apartments until they can find a place of their own. Frequently some of these families move in and out as their situations change. Both the temporary visitors and the host family or friends experience a number of stressors. Insufficient space, lack of privacy, and worries about the landlord's reaction and possible eviction top the list.

Current Status of the Intervention: A unit of field work students in the local university's School of Social Work has been assigned to a community-based agency. Their field work involves working with staff to address homelessness in Bangor. Based on a preliminary assessment of the community, the staff and students have decided to establish a community coalition to address the need for services in the county. The preliminary assessment identified a small number of agencies that are already working with this population but also revealed major gaps in the continuum of services. The proposed coalition will facilitate communication among agencies already delivering services and encourage a more coherent and coordinated response from these agencies and other potential partners to the problems the more invisible population of homeless individuals and families are experiencing.

Initial Charge to the Task Force: The coalition will begin by considering the following issues and developing a preliminary action plan:

⊙ Raising awareness of the problem among agencies and the community at large about the scope of the problem;

⊙ Exploring a range of alternative responses (e.g., new and expanded emergency shelters, increasing low income housing options from already existing property at the former army base)

⊙ Considering improved ways of coordinating existing services for people who are homeless (e.g., shared computerized databases).

Group Tasks:

1. Identify the key players who should be invited to join the task force. Give the rationale for these choices.

2. Evaluate the goals. Modify the list by adding and/or subtracting goals. Give the rationale for the final list of goals.

POTENTIAL TASK FORCE MEMBERS: The following list was devised at the initial meeting of those interested in homelessness in Bangor. The list is not complete; other agencies may be added as the organizing group sees fit.

- ⊙ **BANGOR PUBLIC HOUSING AUTHORITY:** Low-income housing developments scattered throughout the greater Bangor area. Serves families experiencing poverty, some single parents, some teen parents.

- ⊙ **BANGOR COMMUNITY EMERGENCY SHELTER:** A program serving primarily individuals, primarily men, without housing. Short term shelter stays. Some linkage with programs offering more permanent solutions to homelessness.

- ⊙ **GREATER BANGOR CHURCH ALLIANCE:** A consortium of churches providing various types of assistance on an ad hoc basis.

- ⊙ **DOROTHEA DIX EMERGENCY MENTAL HEALTH PROGRAM:** A program providing emergency intervention for persons with chronic mental illness. Serves primarily adults, but is developing a program for adolescents.

- ⊙ **LOAVES AND FISHES FOOD PANTRIES OF GREATER BANGOR:** A loosely connected group of food pantries and soup kitchens supported primarily by Protestant churches. Provide emergency food assistance to area people on an as-needed basis.

- ⊙ **PENOBSCOT BUSINESS ASSOCIATION:** An alliance of business owners and managers from the Greater Bangor Area. Several owners of large apartment buildings are members.

- ⊙ **PENOBSCOT MEDIATION SERVICES:** A program providing short-term intervention for families experiencing difficulties either in the community with neighbors or internally with family members.

- ⊙ **ROBICHAUD HOUSE:** A program serving homeless teens. Primarily provides overnight accommodations, but has little space or staff of daytime programming.

- ⊙ **TENANTS ASSOCIATION OF PENOBSCOT COUNTY:** Provides a variety of services relating to tenants' rights.

Source: From Alexander, G. (1996). Project homeless. In R.F. Rivas & G.H. Hull, Jr. *Case studies in generalist practice*. Pacific Grove, CA: Brooks/Cole Publishing Co., p. 133. Adapted with permission from the author.

ACTIVITY 3-13: Illustrating case and class advocacy – *Erin Brockovich* [Rated R]

IN THE CLASSROOM: Viewing *Erin Brockovich* will help you to distinguish between case and class advocacy. The film illustrates some of the principles of community-based advocacy covered in your readings.

IN THE FIELD: *Erin Brockovich* and the accompanying discussion are suitable for use in training workshops with community-based advocates, for staff in-service training, or for professional development workshops. Using the Practitioner's Notes as a guide, reflect on ways you might use this film in your field placement or in your future professional practice?

MATERIALS: Readings on advocacy [e.g., Chapter 14 - Advocacy. In K.K. Kirst-Ashman & G.H. Hull, Jr. (2002). *Understanding generalist practice (3rd ed.)*. Pacific Grove, CA: Brooks/Cole, pp. 473-495; Class Advocacy. In B.W. Sheafor, C.R. Horejsi, & G.A. Horejsi. (1997). *Techniques and guidelines for social work practice (4th ed.)*, pp.552-555], VCR, TV, videotape, viewing instructions.

GROUP SIZE: 30-40

TIME REQUIRED: Viewing time outside class or time to show clips comparing case and class advocacy and illustrating the development of community-based advocacy.

SPACE REQUIREMENTS: Classroom to view the video and to hold a class discussion.

PREPARATION: Complete the assigned readings and be prepared to participate in a discussion of the content before viewing the video.

INSTRUCTIONS:

The session before the large group discussion: Read the instructions and the Viewing Guide below. Raise any questions or points needing clarification. Obtain a copy of the video or make arrangements to view the film with classmates. Independently select portions of the video that you think illustrate key points relating to case and class advocacy and to effective community organizing (e.g., comparison of interviewing styles between Erin and Theresa, use of the community meetings, negotiating with representatives of P.G. & E, door to door work, apparently serendipitous meeting with Charles Embry).

The discussion: Using the viewing guide as a framework, you will participate in a discussion of the scenes in the video illustrating key points in the readings on advocacy. When the viewing guide topics are exhausted, you will be asked to draw out the implications for social work practice, and you may be asked to help summarize the discussion.

PRACTITIONER'S NOTES:

- At what stage(s) of group development would this activity be useful?

- How would member's characteristics, skills, and abilities influence the way you would modify and implement this activity?

·   How would this activity contribute to the group goals, members' goals, and session goals?

·   At what point in the group meeting would you introduce the activity?

·   How would you evaluate the usefulness and impact of the activity on the group and its members?

INSTRUCTIONS AND VIEWING GUIDE - *Erin Brockovich*

Instructions: View the video using the Viewing Guide below. Identify and note scenes in the video that illustrate case and class advocacy and elements of advocacy skills demonstrated by the interactions between the members of the law firms and the residents of Hinckley. Note implications for social work practice in community-based advocacy. Be prepared to discuss the video in the next session, applying content from the readings to relevant scenes from the video.

Viewing Guide: Identify scenes from the video that illustrate the following:

⊙   Interviewing skills:

⊙   Negotiating skills:

⊙   Case advocacy:

⊙   Evolution to class advocacy:

⊙   Strategies for working in the community:

⊙   Implications for practice:

⊙   Other relevant issues:

Chapter 4
Supervision and In-Service Training

SUPERVISION AND IN-SERVICE TRAINING

This chapter focuses on issues in group supervision, especially culturally sensitive practice, and on one of the central responsibilities of the supervisor and worker—program evaluation. These topics are frequently covered in foundation generalist practice courses. The activities included in this chapter offer you ways to enhance and reinforce the content you have read on these two subjects. The first four activities explore aspects of group supervision. These activities work equally well either in professional development workshops for supervisors working to improve their skills in group supervision or for staff in-service training. The component, *In the Field*, discusses various practice applications for each activity to help you to transfer the strategies and techniques from the classroom to the practice setting.

Activity A 4-1 *The Herb/Zen Desk Gardening* introduces you to the notion that supervisory support can be expanded beyond verbal interventions and can have an impact not just on an individual staff member's circumstances but on the office environment as a whole. The horticultural therapy literature is replete with uses of plants and gardening to reduce stress and increase well being in social services (see references on Horticulture in the Resource Bibliography). Furthermore, making connections beyond the spoken word and having fun making the desk gardens together can enhance the working relationships in the supervision group between the supervisor and staff and among staff members. Similarly, A 4-2 *Images* relies on movement, sharing physical space, observation, and collaboration rather than on the more traditional group discussion. In this activity, you will communicate your perceptions of and assumptions about professional self-image through a group collage by writing those perceptions on a life-size outline of a person drawn on a large piece of paper. Although discussion follows, the central component of the activity is the artistic expression of each class member's perceptions.

Skill in working with diverse populations is central to competent generalist social work practice. The following activities will assist you first in exploring your own cultural background and then in moving on to compare and contrast your experiences with those of others who may be very similar or vastly different from you. The first activity on this topic, A 4-3 *Cultural Self-Awareness*, asks you to examine your cultural roots and to reflect on the way your background has influenced your life both positively and negatively. Both A 4-4 *Fallout Shelter* and A 4-5 *Culturally Influenced Behaviors* focus on assumptions, prejudices, and discriminatory behavior (both positive and negative) that exist in everyone. The next two activities move you from reflection to action. In A 4-6 *Making Changes* you will make conscious and specific plans to improve your knowledge, understanding, and experience of some population that is different from you and to challenge your preconceptions about them.

In A 4-9 *Issues in Cross-cultural Supervision—Part One* and A 4-10 *Issues in Cross-cultural Supervision—Part Two* assist you in thinking about the role culture plays in agency administration, and, by extension, in the provision of direct services to the community. It can help raise a difficult subject in a relatively non-threatening way. In

A 4-14 *Developing Role-play Scenarios*, you will take responsibility for raising practice issues or topics for discussion. The role-play scenarios function as discussion starters. This activity expands the possibilities for supervision and reinforces the idea that staff members and supervisors are both responsible for the effectiveness and success of the supervisory process. I developed these three activities first as training tools in working with groups of supervisors in various venues nationally and locally and subsequently have used them with both BSW and MSW students as well.

The last two activities augment course content on evaluation of social work practice with groups. In A 4-15 *Evaluation of Practice,* students work in small groups to develop plans for documenting and evaluating program effectiveness in group services. In the agency setting, this activity has been used in staff in-service training either to brainstorm more effective approaches to record keeping or to help introduce changes in recording and management of data on service provision.

Some of the exercises in this chapter employ fairly traditional educational methods—group discussion, guided experiential activities, and written work. By contrast, the last five activities capitalize on popular music as a reflection of society with respect to ethnicity, gender, and age. A 4-7 *Carefully Taught* and A 4-8 *Black, Brown, and White Blues* mirror societal attitudes toward race and ethnicity. A 4-11 *Soliloquy* and A 4-13 *I'm Gonna Be an Engineer* explore gender issues and the benefits/consequences of straying from traditional gender roles. A 4-12 *Officer Krupke* looks at urban teenage boys from multiple perspectives—the social worker, the judge, and the policeman on the beat. Beyond the lyrics, the music conveys mood and speaks to typical feelings that surround each issue. Both the music and the lyrics convey something about our cultural context. Consider ways you might incorporate music into your work with groups. You might also think about activities other than just listening. What changes might occur in a group that sings, plays simple instruments, or writes songs together?

As in previous sections, ways to bridge the distance between the educational setting to the practice world appear in the component, *In the Field*. This approach increases the versatility of the exercises and provides you as a beginning social work practitioner with a compendium of program activities for use in the field placement and in generalist practice with groups.

ACTIVITY 4-1: Herbal/Zen Desk Gardening

IN THE CLASSROOM: Making a desk garden will help you to explore a strategy for coping with stress and enhancing the work environment in your field placement.

IN THE FIELD: You might use this activity in your staff group supervision or for a staff in-service training session where the focus is on ways to manage stress in the workplace. If your office has outdoor space, you could expand this activity to create the Herb and/or Zen garden in a courtyard or secluded corner with a bench or two for staff and clients to use in learning about stress reduction techniques. To simplify the activity, create only one of the gardens. The Zen garden is the simpler of the two, requiring only a shallow container with a lid for transporting it safely, sand, rocks, and a fork for raking the patterns. To convert the activity to a single project for the group to create for the office or agency, select a larger container that can be kept in a central location such as the staff lounge where staff members can enjoy it during break time or in a supervised location if you make it available to agency clients. A larger, two-section container allows for more plants in the soil section. Indoor potted plants may be substituted for growing herbs.

Small container gardening is also a useful activity with all age groups, from pre-schoolers planting and caring for beans in a cup to youth and adults creating the more complex Herb/Zen garden. Container gardening can serve as a metaphor for a range of life issues—nurturing and being nurtured, dealing with loss when a plant dies, as a normalizing activity that helps participate in a hobby enjoyed by young and old alike, or as a way to work either independently or with others to complete a task. When you are using this activity in your practice setting, you should make a sample garden either using seeds or small herb or house plants. Note areas where difficulties may arise. Adjust the activity or the instructions to remedy the problem areas. Use the Practitioner's Notes to consider ways you could use this activity with other groups in your field practice setting.

MATERIALS: One to two large bags of potting soil in plastic buckets with lids and handles; 10-12 two-compartment plastic food containers with lids and enough depth to accommodate small plants; one package of plastic forks; one package of craft sticks; several packages of easily germinated seeds; two gallons of sand in a plastic bucket with lid and handle; 1 gallon container of water with screw-top lids and handle; a roll of paper towels; thin-tipped permanent markers; paper cups for scooping soil, sand, water; three rocks per student; enough newspaper or plastic drop cloths to cover the work space; broom, dustpan and brush, waste basket for clean up. A photo of a Zen garden for illustration (optional).

GROUP SIZE: 12 maximum

TIME REQUIRED: 45 minutes to one hour, including set up and clean up time.

SPACE REQUIREMENTS: Enough table or floor space for the class to plant the gardens.

PREPARATION: Before the session where the activity will occur, the instructor will give you a list of items you will need to purchase and/or gather. The class members will help the instructor to prepare the room, spreading the newspaper or drop cloth(s) over the workspace. Locate the potting soil, sand, and water containers so that they are easily accessible for class members to scoop into the plastic garden dishes with minimum spillage. Some herbs, plants, and/or the dust from sand or soil may cause allergic reactions. Be sure to alert the instructor before the activity if you have an allergy.

INSTRUCTIONS: The instructor will facilitate a discussion on the topic of stress. You should be prepared to suggest ways that you think might reduce stress in the school and/or field setting. View the photo of a Zen garden if the instructor has brought one to illustrate this part of the discussion.

To create the garden, you will begin by placing the sand in one compartment of the container, filling it to no more than a half inch from the top. Next fill the remaining half of the container with potting soil, again leaving at least a half-inch from the top. You can begin the planting process at your workspace, planting seeds in the potting soil and placing the rocks in the sand. Select a few of the types of seeds available (3-4 different types maximum, depending on the size of the container), write the name of each on a craft stick using the marker. Place the seeds on a paper towel next to the appropriately labeled craft stick. Plant the seeds in the soil, inserting the craft stick label in the soil where those seeds have been planted. When you have planted all the seeds, return to the table with the water container and pour a small amount in your paper cup to water the soil lightly. Return to your workspace and place the rocks on the sand in an artistic pattern. Draw the fork through the sand to make a simple design (e.g., a figure eight, a whorl beginning in the center of the garden and spiraling out to the edge. Cover the garden with the lid to make it ready to transport. Be sure it stays level to avoid spilling and mixing the sand and the soil. Once you get it to your office, lift the cover and let it rest loosely on the top of the soil to create a greenhouse effect to promote propagation of the seeds. When the leaves begin to sprout, remove the cover to let them grow. Water the garden lightly and regularly according to the instructions on the seed packets, making sure the garden has a good light source as well.

PRACTITIONER'S NOTES:

- With what types of groups would you use this activity?

- At what stage(s) of group development would this activity be useful?

- How would member's characteristics, skills, and abilities influence the way you would modify and implement this activity?

- How would this activity contribute to the group goals, members' goals, and session goals?

- At what point in the group meeting would you introduce the activity?

·   How would you evaluate the usefulness and impact of the activity on the group and its
    members?

Source: From *The Zen-Healing Desk Garden*, an activity analysis created by Audrie Staples for a
course assignment in SWK 597 – Horticultural Therapy Methods I, University of Maine
School of Social Work, Spring 2001, Elin MacKinnon, Instructor.

ACTIVITY 4-2: Images

IN THE CLASSROOM: In *Images* you will explore the elements of your professional self-image and examine the similarities and differences among class members' perceptions of being a professional social worker.

IN THE FIELD: You might use this activity as a discussion starter in agency group supervision, in small groups in staff in-service training or professional development workshops. *Images* may also be used in groups from school-age children through adults where the topic focuses on views of one's self and, by extension, the ways others view us. The suggested variations allow for greater or lesser direct involvement of the group members, making the activity adaptable for various stages of group development and various levels of self-disclosure and participation. The less cohesive the group, the lower the demand for self-disclosure and participation should be. For example, if you are working with a group in the early stages of group development, using the previously prepared outline of a generic person allows members to engage in the activity with a greater degree of comfort than asking group members to pose for making personal outlines. This approach would also be indicated if one or more group members is a survivor of physical abuse. *Images* may be repeated at succeeding points in the life of the group to note the way perceptions of self-image change and evolve. Each member might keep a folder of individual work, or you might keep the group collages for reuse at various stages of group development

If the wall space is limited, you can replace the large image with a smaller image duplicated on 11"x14" paper. Members would then complete individual self-images using markers to write or draw key aspects in the outlined figure. Depending on the stage of group development, the group could contribute the individual images to a collage assembled on the wall and then proceed with the discussion. Rather than use markers to write or draw, you can use magazines and other materials, scissors, and glue sticks to create either a group or individual collage. If the group is in the intimacy or differentiation stage of group development, you might ask members to draw each other's outlines on large pieces of paper, creating full-size, self-images.

MATERIALS: Two large sheets of thick paper, approximately 6 feet long by 3 feet wide; markers.

GROUP SIZE: 6-12

TIME REQUIRED: 30 minutes.

SPACE REQUIREMENTS: Classroom with enough wall space to tape the paper vertically; chairs arranged in a circle so that the paper can be seen easily from each chair.

PREPARATION: The instructor will assemble the equipment. Using one of the sheets, one student will volunteer to draw the outline of another student on the large sheet of paper using a thick, brightly colored marker. Tape the two sheets of paper firmly to the wall at the top, bottom, and sides. The bottom sheet should protect the wall from any of the markers soaking through the top sheet. Run a trial with two layers of scrap sheets to make sure the wall is protected.

INSTRUCTIONS: Each class member will select a marker. You will write or draw aspects of professional self-image from your perspective on the outlined figure. When everyone has written at least one item, step back from your work and contemplate what you each have written and/or drawn. Add any elements that you think may be missing. Be seated in the circle when you think the work is complete. Using the items included in the outline as a springboard, participate in a discussion of what being a professional social worker means. Using the Practitioner's Notes as a guide, consider other ways you might incorporate this activity into your practice with groups.

PRACTITIONER'S NOTES:

·   With what types of groups would you use this activity?

·   At what stage(s) of group development would this activity be useful?

·   How would member's characteristics, skills, and abilities influence the way you would modify and implement this activity?

·   How would this activity contribute to the group goals, members' goals, and session goals?

·   At what point in the group meeting would you introduce the activity?

·   How would you evaluate the usefulness and impact of the activity on the group and its members?

ACTIVITY 4-3: Cultural Self-Awareness

IN THE CLASSROOM: The *Cultural Self-Awareness* activity will give you an opportunity to explore and clarify the meaning of your cultural background in a personal way and to understand the commonalities and differences among class members.

IN THE FIELD: You can adapt this activity as an oral history project for groups of children of middle school age through groups of adults. Group members might create posters with family photos, maps of the country of origin, maps showing the immigration routes, and other artifacts from their cultural heritage. Some members may consider themselves Americans with little or no ties to a culture of origin. You can encourage group members to look at the region of the U.S. where their families have roots and present those findings.

You can also adapt the activity to focus on a particular aspect of members' cultural backgrounds. For example, the group could explore spirituality. The topics in this adaptation might include:

(a) Identify your family's religious origins as far back as you can. Identify specifics relating to family of origin religious practices as far back as you have current knowledge. Note the changes in religious affiliation, if any.

(b) Identify the strengths and disadvantages of your religious background.

(c) Consider how your current faith/spirituality/religious affiliation(s) are similar to and different from your earlier years.

(d) In one or two sentences, name your religious background, and describe one important personal benefit that you enjoy as a consequence.

MATERIALS: Instruction sheet

GROUP SIZE: 30

TIME REQUIRED: Approximately 20 minutes in the week before the next group session; 45 minutes class time—30 minutes for task group, 15 minutes for class discussion.

SPACE REQUIREMENTS: A room large enough to seat students comfortably plus breakout areas for small groups.

PREPARATION: At the session before the activity is to be used, read the instruction sheet, which follows. Consider the importance of developing an understanding of the role culture plays in human development and the centrality of cultural issues in effective professional practice. Raise any questions and points for clarification.

INSTRUCTIONS: At the session where the activity will be used, divide into task groups of five to six members. Each group will select a reporter who will share the results of the task group's discussion with the class. You will have 30 minutes to share the sentences each of you has written. Note similarities and differences among the members of your group. As a group, prepare the summary for the report-back. The instructor will be available for consultation as needed. Move to the breakout area assigned to your group and complete the steps for the activity as outlined above. Reconvene as a class and proceed with the reports. Note similarities and differences among the task group reports to contribute to the discussion that will follow the reports. Explore the relevance for professional practice.

PRACTIONER'S NOTES:

· With what types of groups would you use this activity?

· At what stage(s) of group development would this activity be useful?

· How would member's characteristics, skills, and abilities influence the way you would modify and implement this activity?

· How would this activity contribute to the group goals, members' goals, and session goals?

· At what point in the group meeting would you introduce the activity?

· How would you evaluate the usefulness and impact of the activity on the group and its members?

CULTURAL SELF-AWARENESS

INSTRUCTIONS:

I. Sometime before the next meeting, please take 20 minutes to do this section individually without discussion with other class members.

> (a) Identify your family origins as far back as you can trace specific ancestors. Where possible, specify the earliest dates, names, and places of which you can be sure. If you are unsure, speculate about probable ancestors and how far back you might be able to trace them, as though you were planning to do genealogical research.

> (b) If your ancestors are not Native American, why and how did they (or you, if you are a first generation immigrant) come to this country? Speculate on the conditions they left behind and on possible circumstances or motives for leaving these conditions?

> (c) Your ancestors' cultural background undoubtedly influenced how they were perceived and treated by others. Write down both a disadvantage and an advantage your ancestors may have experienced because of their background. Examples might include matters of religion, ethnic and/or racial characteristics, economic background, language, family patterns, or political involvement.

> (d) Look at any of the advantages you have listed. These are often reflected in family strengths, the desirable things people do or experience because they are members of a particular family and a particular cultural group. Can you name any specific privileges, advantages, or family strengths that you or your family members have enjoyed because of your family's cultural background or identity? List these.

> (e) In one or two sentences, name your cultural background, and describe one important personal benefit that you enjoy as a consequence.

> (f) Bring your notes to the task group session.

II. At the designated time, class will be divided into small task groups of five to six students. Select a reporter to share the results of your discussion with the group. The small groups will take 15 minutes to share the sentences each member has written. Use the remaining 15 minutes to discuss similarities and differences among task group member's backgrounds. Prepare a summary of the task group's findings for the reporter to bring to the class discussion.

III. Report back/Discussion (15 minutes)

NOTES:

Source: From James W. Green, J.W. *Cultural awareness in the human services*. Published by Allyn and Bacon, Boston, MA. Copyright 1982 by Pearson Education. Reprinted by permission of the publisher.

ACTIVITY 4-4: Fallout Shelter

IN THE CLASSROOM: The *Fallout Shelter* activity will raise your awareness of assumptions and biases that may occur in your decision-making processes in the practice setting.

IN THE FIELD: You might use the *Fallout Shelter* with middle-school children through adults to stimulate discussion of inclusion/exclusion from groups, stereotyping, and scapegoating. The description of the candidates for inclusion/exclusion should be altered to fit the purpose of the session and to be relevant to the demographics of the group's membership. You can also substitute other scenarios for the Fall Out Shelter (e.g., Marooned on a Desert Island, Lost at Sea, Snowbound in Antarctica, or other situations where groups are faced with forced choices). On rare occasions, some group members have found this exercise threatening based on past personal experience and opted not to participate, offering to discuss the issues instead of completing the decision-making task. You should consider carefully whether that alternative would meet the goals for the session and the purpose of the activity, given the composition of the group.

MATERIALS: Activity sheet given below.

GROUP SIZE: 30

TIME REQUIRED: 20 minutes

SPACE REQUIREMENTS: A classroom large enough to seat students in a circle plus small meeting areas for breakout groups.

PREPARATION: Review the activity instructions given below and raise any relevant questions. Note, however, that no further information on the candidates is available. The task groups must make decisions using the descriptions as written.

INSTRUCTIONS: Divide into small groups. You will meet for 15 minutes. The groups will choose a reporter, and make their selections. The small groups must make their decisions fairly quickly using whatever decision-making processes they find most useful. The class will reconvene, and the groups will report their decisions and the rationales they used in making their selections. A debriefing on the exercise will follow the reports.

PRACTITIONER'S NOTES:

· With what types of groups would you use this activity?

· At what stage(s) of group development would this activity be useful?

· How would member's characteristics, skills, and abilities influence the way you would modify and implement this activity?

·   How would this activity contribute to the group goals, members' goals, and session goals?

·   At what point in the group meeting would you introduce the activity?

·   How would you evaluate the usefulness and impact of the activity on the group and its members?

FALLOUT SHELTER

INSTRUCTIONS: You and your group have been selected to be part of the post Nuclear Power Plant accident survival population. Your group is to select *five and only five* additional people to share your shelter for a minimum of three years. The space in the shelter will be very limited. Sleeping quarters will be dormitory style. The people listed below have been assigned to your group as candidates to be included in your shelter. The information given below is all that is available on the candidates. Those not selected face certain and painful death.

1.   A 16 year old Hispanic who has dropped out of high school and is pregnant. Known to be hostile and throw temper tantrums.

2.   A 39 year old former prostitute who retired from the business four years ago.

3.   A 36 year old physician educated in South Africa. Known to be unable to have children. A well-known and very vocal segregationist.

4.   A 35 year old commercial architect and an open homosexual.

5.   A 46 year old Haitian plumber on parole. Served seven years for trafficking cocaine and heroin.

6.   A profoundly deaf, 20 year old African American. Certified electrician.

7.   An Asian ex-police officer with an arsenal of weapons. Recently discharged from the force because of excessive brutality on the job. Convicted of spouse abuse.

8.   A 54 year old minister in a wheelchair because of a spinal cord injury from a car accident three years ago. Never married.

9.   A brilliant 26 year old law student. Trained survivalist; refuses to be separated from spouse.

10. Spouse of the law student. Past history of psychiatric hospitalizations. Refuses to be separated from spouse.

Source: Adapted from TABLE 1. Fall-Out Shelter Exercise in B. Rittner and M. Nakanishi (1993). Challenging stereotypes and cultural biases. *Social Work with Groups, 16*(4), p. 13. Copyright 1993, Haworth Press, Inc., Binghamton, NY. Article copies available from the Haworth Document Delivery Service: 1-800-HAWORTH. E-mail address: getinfo@haworthpressinc.com Used with permission.

ACTIVITY 4-5: Culturally Influenced Behavior

IN THE CLASSROOM: This activity aims to heighten your awareness of your cultural background and assumptions you make about the domains included on the form. It is a means of increasing self-awareness about the ways your own cultural background and the ways it influences your thinking and behavior. Furthermore the self-reflection you will complete in this activity will help to inform your work with diverse population groups.

IN THE FIELD: You can use this activity with middle-schoolers through adults. It may be best used at the intimacy phase of group development to promote group cohesion and an understanding of similarities and differences in thinking and approach. Depending on the focus of the group, you can alter the domains to suit that emphasis. For example, this exercise can be renamed *Attitudes as Influenced by Religious Background* and adapted for a discussion of spirituality. The focus shifts to the sayings or practices members were taught as children based on their religious or spiritual upbringing. You would ask the group members to recall typical sayings they heard from family members or religious/spiritual leaders. The domains in this variation might include: family, women, children, authority, health, self-reliance, persons outside the spiritual group, personal success, financial responsibility. When using this variation, homogeneous groups based on religious affiliation or spiritual practice work will promote a lively discussion of within group and across group variations.

MATERIALS: Newsprint, thick markers, masking tape.

GROUP SIZE: 30

TIME REQUIRED: 1 hour

SPACE REQUIREMENTS: A classroom large enough to accommodate the students in a circle plus small areas for breakout groups; wall space to post the newsprint lists from the small groups.

PREPARATION: The instructor will assemble the materials listed above, arrange chairs in a circle, and check wall space for posting newsprint. You will read the *Culturally Influenced Behaviors* form given below and raise any questions you have.

INSTRUCTIONS:

Small Group Discussion (Ω hr.)—The class will divide into small groups composed homogeneously by ethnic identification. Occasionally, some class members have difficulty identifying an ethnic group connection with their family history and may consider themselves Americans with little or no ties to a previous culture of origin. If you fall into this category, you might consider the region of the U.S. where your family has roots and form a group based on regional affiliation. In the small groups, you will complete the *Culturally Influenced Behaviors* forms individually. When everyone has finished the form, compare what you each wrote. On the newsprint, write (in letters large and dark enough to read across the room) one or two sayings that most closely identify the sayings typical of this ethnic/cultural group for each of the six domains. Bring the newsprint back to the main room to tape up on the wall. The instructor will be available during the task group activity for consultation on an as-needed basis.

Large Group Observation/Discussion (1/2 hr.)—When the class reconvenes, each group will tape up their sayings on the wall space provided. The class members will take five minutes walk around the room to read what other groups have written for each of the six domains. You should note the similarities and differences among the groups. You then will be seated in a circle and discuss your observations noting similarities and differences among and within groups. Consider the potential impact on work with clients. Reflect on the importance of this data for your work with clients and colleagues.

PRACTITIONER'S NOTES:

- With what types of groups would you use this activity?

- At what stage(s) of group development would this activity be useful?

- How would member's characteristics, skills, and abilities influence the way you would modify and implement this activity?

- How would this activity contribute to the group goals, members' goals, and session goals?

- At what point in the group meeting would you introduce the activity?

- How would you evaluate the usefulness and impact of the activity on the group and its members?

CULTURALLY INFLUENCED BEHAVIORS

INSTRUCTIONS: Recall sayings you were taught as a child. In the space provided, record one or two sayings for each domain, even if you no longer behave the way you were taught was the "right way" to think or to do things. Typical sayings might include "Time is money;" "The early bird catches the worm;" "A woman's place is in the home."

1. Help Seeking Behavior:

2. Medical Care and Illness:

3. Gender Roles:

4. Role of Family:

5. Behavior toward Authority:

6. Time and Punctuality:

Source: Adapted from TABLE 2. Domains Culturally Influenced Behaviors: A Descriptive Grid in B. Rittner and M. Nakanishi (1993). Challenging stereotypes and cultural biases. *Social Work with Groups, 16*(4), p. 19. Copyright 1993, Haworth Press, Inc., Binghamton, NY. Article copies available from the Haworth Document Delivery Service: 1-800-HAWORTH. E-mail address: getinfo@haworthpressinc.com Used with permission.

ACTIVITY 4-6: Making Changes—Steps toward Cultural Competence

IN THE CLASSROOM: In this activity you will put your learning about cultural issues into practice and work to increase your level of cultural awareness and competence.

IN THE FIELD: You might use similar letter writing activities in practice settings to focus group members on transferring learning and experiences within the group setting to their lives outside the group. Depending on the maturity level of group members, you may become the person to hold the letters for the final session. Using the *Practitioner's Notes*, think about ways you might adapt this activity to your groups in your field placement or future practice setting.

MATERIALS: Letter forms and envelopes.

GROUP SIZE: 30-40

TIME REQUIRED: 10 minutes

SPACE REQUIREMENTS: Sufficient table or desk space for students to write the letter privately.

PREPARATION: The instructor will duplicate the letter form given below and bring the forms and envelopes to the class session.

INSTRUCTIONS: Using the envelope and paper provided, write a letter to yourself identifying:

1. A learning activity you will undertake in the next week to improve your level of cultural awareness. Include date by which the activity will occur.

2. An interpersonal activity you will complete in the next month to increase your cultural competence. Include date.

3. A series of learning and interpersonal activities in which you will engage to enhance your cultural competence during the period designated by the instructor. Include dates.

4. Seal the letter in the envelope and address it to yourself. Date the letter in the stamp corner with "FINAL SESSION". Exchange letters with someone in class. Return the letter to that person on the last day of the group.

5. The class will use 5-10 minutes of the final session to debrief the activity, using material from volunteers willing to discuss their attempts to enhance their level of cultural competence. Volunteers should be prepared to report on both successful and less satisfactory experiences and to reflect on what they learned in each situation.

PRACTITIONER'S NOTES:

· With what types of groups would you use this activity?

· At what stage(s) of group development would this activity be useful?

· How would member's characteristics, skills, and abilities influence the way you would modify and implement this activity?

· How would this activity contribute to the group goals, members' goals, and session goals?

· At what point in the group meeting would you introduce the activity?

· How would you evaluate the usefulness and impact of the activity on the group and its members?

ACTIVITY 4-7: Illustrating the Development of Racial Prejudice–*Carefully Taught*

IN THE CLASSROOM: Listening to and discussing *Carefully Taught* will help you to think about the ways racial prejudice develops and how it has an impact on social work practice.

IN THE FIELD: Lyrics from songs such as *Carefully Taught* are useful in introducing difficult topics in a low-key, relatively non-threatening way in situations where you want to raise prejudice and discrimination as topics for discussion and issues for behavior change. Be sure to prepare two or three questions to use in jumpstarting the discussion following the playing of the tape. You can use this activity with group members from school age through adults. You can encourage the group to reflect on the attitudes and behaviors expressed by the performer, make connections with circumstances in the group or in the community where the group exists, and move on to consider strategies for addressing problem areas. If you are involved in planning staff in-service training or conducting workshops on cross-cultural issues in the community, you might use *Carefully Taught* as a useful discussion starter. If *South Pacific* is available on video and the group has access to a video player, cue the tape to the performance of *Carefully Taught*, view the video, and proceed with the discussion. In groups where members may have hearing difficulties, use a transcript of the lyrics. If group members have visual constraints, the audiotape is obviously preferable to the video.

Beyond discussion, you can spin off a variety of activities from the song lyrics depending on the age, interests, and skills of the group. For example, you might use the song as a basis for a skit or puppet show illustrating how prejudiced attitudes and stereotyping can be transmitted. The group might also create a large wall display printing key lines from the song on large sheets of paper and illustrate them as posters.

MATERIALS: Tape recorder, tape; CD, CD player; or VCR, TV, and tape of *South Pacific*.

GROUP SIZE: 30

TIME REQUIRED: 15 minutes

SPACE REQUIREMENTS: A classroom where students can be seated close enough to hear the recording easily.

PREPARATION: The instructor will assemble and check the equipment.

INSTRUCTIONS: Listen intently to the song, noting the ways prejudice develops and persists. Contribute your responses to what you heard to the discussion. Compare the experiences in the lyrics to your own experiences with or observations about prejudice and discrimination. When that topic has been exhausted, move to considering the potential impact of prejudice and discrimination on practice situations, particularly those associated with your field placement.

PRACTITIONER'S NOTES:

·   With what types of groups would you use this activity?

·   At what stage(s) of group development would this activity be useful?

·   How would member's characteristics, skills, and abilities influence the way you would modify and implement this activity?

·   How would this activity contribute to the group goals, members' goals, and session goals?

·   At what point in the group meeting would you introduce the activity?

·   How would you evaluate the usefulness and impact of the activity on the group and its members?

Resources: The soundtrack from *South Pacific* is readily available from sources on the web (e.g. ProMusicFind.com) and may also be available in local library CD and tape collections.

ACTIVITY 4-8: Illustrating Racial Discrimination—
Black, Brown, and White Blues

IN THE CLASSROOM: This recording, *Black, Brown, and White Blues*, will help you think about prejudice and discrimination based on skin color and the impact of this behavior on practice.

IN THE FIELD: *Black, Brown, and White Blues* is another resource that is useful for introducing difficult topics associated with prejudice and discrimination in a novel and less threatening way. Group members from older school age children and youth through adults can comment on attitudes and behaviors expressed by the performer, make connections with circumstances in the group, in the community where the group resides, and/or with personal experiences. You can help group members to devise strategies for addressing inequities based on skin color and ways to interrupt the resulting oppression.

Beyond discussion, you and the group can spin off a variety of activities based on the song lyrics. For example, the group might use the song as a basis for a skit creating situations suggested in the lyrics. You might have the group create a series of posters with the printed lyrics by having three task groups create drawings or collages illustrating the differential treatment each of the three populations received as described in the song. Other task groups could design additional posters illustrating possible remedies for discriminatory practices.

You may broaden the discussion by using additional songs (e.g., lyrics from *One* by Creed on reverse discrimination and *The Way It Is* by Bruce Hornsby, both found on the Web at ecell2.k12.us/2001/projects/mohs3/SongsLyrics/independet.htm). In groups where members have hearing difficulties, you should prepare a transcript of the lyrics for group members.

MATERIALS: Tape recorder, tape

GROUP SIZE: 30

TIME REQUIRED: 15 minutes

SPACE REQUIREMENTS: A classroom with seating close enough for students to hear the recording easily.

PREPARATION: The instructor will assemble and check the equipment.

INSTRUCTIONS: Listen intently to the song, making notes on the differential treatment the performer describes. Using your notes, participate in a discussion that will explore prejudice and discrimination based on skin color. Consider whether color is a visual cue that is as powerful today as it has been in the past. Think about whether such prejudice and discrimination is an historical phenomenon only or whether it persists today. Be prepared to defend you position with examples. When these topics have been exhausted, move on to discuss the potential impact on your practice.

PRACTITIONER'S NOTES:

- At what stage(s) of group development would this activity be useful?

- How would member's characteristics, skills, and abilities influence the way you would modify and implement this activity?

- How would this activity contribute to the group goals, members' goals, and session goals?

- At what point in the group meeting would you introduce the activity?

- How would you evaluate the usefulness and impact of the activity on the group and its members?

Source: *Black, Brown, White Blues* is available on *Carry It On* by Pete Seeger, Jane Sapp, and Si Kahn, issued by Flying Fish Records and available from on-line booksellers (e.g., Barnes&Noble.com).

ACTIVITY 4-9: Issues in Cross-cultural Supervision, Part One – The Vignette and Discussion

IN THE CLASSROOM: In this activity you will apply your assessment and problem-solving skills to the tasks of supervision in a cross-cultural setting.

IN THE FIELD: You might use this activity in peer group supervision and in professional development workshops of any size. You can vary the focus and content of the vignette to explore other issues in supervision. You could ask the group members to submit issues for discussion and create vignettes tailored to their interests and concerns.

MATERIALS: Instruction sheets; flip chart and markers or blackboard, chalk, and eraser.

GROUP SIZE: 30-40

TIME REQUIRED: 50 minutes.

SPACE REQUIREMENTS: Classroom plus small breakout areas.

PREPARATION: Before the discussion session, read the vignette and instruction sheet. Raise any points needing further clarification. Make your notes for the discussion.

INSTRUCTIONS: Divide into task groups of four to six members. Each group will act as a peer consultation team that will advise Ms. Reynolds on a possible approach to resolve the supervisory issue(s) presented in the vignette. Each task group will select a recorder/reporter who will present the group's proposed recommendation and rationale for the recommendation to the class. You will have 30 minutes to discuss the vignette, to respond to the questions, and to decide on a recommendation. The instructor will be available for consultation as needed. Go to your group's designated breakout area and complete the task group portion of the activity as outlined in the instructions.

Approximately five minutes before the end of the task group session, conclude the discussion so that you will have time to prepare your recommendation to report to the class discussion. Reconvene as a class. Your group's reporter will present your recommendation and its rationale when your group's turn comes. The instructor will print the solutions on a flip chart or a blackboard. Participate in a discussion comparing and contrasting recommendations. Consider the expected and unintended consequences that may arise for each recommendation.

PRACTITIONER'S NOTES:

· With what types of groups would you use this activity?

· At what stage(s) of group development would this activity be useful?

· How would member's characteristics, skills, and abilities influence the way you would modify and implement this activity?

·   How would this activity contribute to the group goals, members' goals, and session goals?

·   At what point in the group meeting would you introduce the activity?

·   How would you evaluate the usefulness and impact of the activity on the group and its members?

ISSUES IN SUPERVISON PART ONE
Cross-cultural Considerations – The Discussion

INSTRUCTIONS: Before the discussion session, read the following vignette giving the background information for the case example, making notes on your individual responses to the discussion questions. The task groups will discuss the questions and act as a peer consultation team to develop a recommendation for Ms. Reynolds as she addresses the supervisory issues before her.

The Agency: Julia Lathrop Center is a community-based social work agency offering services to families in an ethnically diverse, low-income area of a large city. The agency has an 11-member board of directors composed of three women and eight men. The board has only one minority group member; an African-American woman elected this year. The administrative group includes the executive director, a white woman who has been with the agency for 10 years, and six program supervisors–one African-American man, one Latina, and four white women.

The Current Situation: The Center's executive director has just hired an African-American woman to replace the former program supervisor of the outpost teen parent program. Ms. Reynolds, ACSW, was hired because she has excellent qualifications and has good interpersonal skills, which she demonstrated in a series of interviews. Two not-so-hidden agenda items:

1. Ms. Reynolds was hired, in part, to pacify community complaints. The power structure in the housing project where this outpost program is located is composed mostly of African-American women, though the composition of the community is mixed–African-American, Latino, and Appalachian white.

2. This program has also been having difficulty in controlling the quality of job performance by some of the minority direct service workers. The administration and board hope that the new director will be able to address this issue more effectively than her predecessor.

The Case Example: Ms. Reynolds has been working as program supervisor in the outpost teen parent program for one month. In an effort to get to know the staff, she has occasionally had lunch with the other program supervisors and twice has had lunch with the three minority direct service workers in her program. Generally things are going well, and Ms. Reynolds feels comfortable in her new position.

One problem does loom on the horizon. Ms. Alvarez, the casework supervisor, has just reported that the performance of Ms. Bennett, one of the African-American direct service workers, has not improved since her last unfavorable evaluation three months ago by the previous director who was a white woman. Ms. Bennett, who is a home visitor, complains that the job expectations are both unclear and unrealistic. Ms. Bennett has worked at the local park district program with teens before joining the teen parent program. She is a recent college graduate with a degree in psychology.

The home visitor position as outlined in the written job description requires the following tasks:

- ⊙ teaching basic life skills (child care, money management, housekeeping) to teen mothers in individual counseling sessions usually at the teen's home;

- ⊙ delivering concrete and psychosocial support services (e.g., concrete–trips to public aid; psychosocial–acting as counselor on interpersonal issues);

⊙ record keeping–statistics for the monthly report to the funding agency and logs on service delivery to each program participant;

⊙ taking part in weekly supervision, staff meetings, and staffings on program participants;

⊙ participating in on-going in-service training and continuing education activities.

Ms. Bennett comes to supervision without having submitted her logs to her supervisor, thus derailing the supervision process. She is consistently late with her statistics, causing minor delays in agency reporting to the funder and numerous "headaches" for the program's secretary, Ms. Hernandez. Ms. Bennett has let her co-workers know that she is going to file a grievance against Ms. Alvarez, who has placed her on probation. Ms. Bennett claims that the white and Latina home visitors engage in similar behavior and have not been reprimanded. Ms. Bennett's caseload includes African-American, Latina, and white teen mothers. She always scores high on service evaluations done with program participants.

Discussion Questions:

1. What issues are involved in this supervision problem?

2. What is the main issue for Ms. Reynolds? Why?

3. What steps would you advise Ms. Reynolds to take to resolve the problem?

4. What might be the consequences of such action(s) in relation to:
   ⊙ the board

   ⊙ Ms. Bennett

   ⊙ the executive director

   ⊙ the other home visitors

   ⊙ Ms. Alvarez

   ⊙ the community

ACTIVITY 4-10: Issues in Cross-cultural Supervision, Part Two – The Role-Play

IN THE CLASSROOM: In this activity you will test out the viability of the proposed approaches recommended by each task group in Part One and gain some practice in applying your skills in supervision.

IN THE FIELD: Both the task group discussion and the role-play are useful activities for in-service training or for professional development workshops. If you videotape the role-plays, practitioners participating in the training or workshop can use them to review and critique their application of various supervisory skills and techniques, thereby increasing their skills in reflective practice.

MATERIALS: Recommendations for each task group from Issues in Cross-cultural Supervision, Part I.

GROUP SIZE: 30-40

TIME REQUIRED: 50 minutes.

SPACE REQUIREMENTS: A classroom arranged with an open space for the role-play to be performed and with seating that allows observers a clear view of the action.

PREPARATION: Complete the activities in Part One. Raise any questions and any points needing clarification. Review the instructions below for Part Two. Raise any questions and any points needing clarification. Each group must meet before the next session to work out the details for roles to be played and the general outline of the way the role-play will proceed.

INSTRUCTIONS: Using the plan your group has devised in your out-of-class meeting, your task group will have five minutes to role-play the key point in the encounter between Ms. Reynolds and the staff member(s). Following the role-play, group members should be prepared to present the rationale for their approach in the role-play to the larger group and to discuss the consequences and any unexpected events that may occur in the role-play. After each role-play is completed, the class will engage in a short discussion where those observing will highlight the areas where the proposed solution was effective and any areas where difficulties arose. Then the players will discuss their approach and any unexpected occurrences that arose in the course of the action.

PRACTITIONER'S NOTES:

· With what types of groups would you use this activity?

· At what stage(s) of group development would this activity be useful?

· How would member's characteristics, skills, and abilities influence the way you would modify and implement this activity?

· How would this activity contribute to the group goals, members' goals, and session goals?

· At what point in the group meeting would you introduce the activity?

· How would you evaluate the usefulness and impact of the activity on the group and its members?

ISSUES IN SUPERVISON PART II: Cross-cultural Considerations Role-play

INSTRUCTIONS: Based on the solution derived from your earlier discussion, your task group will have five minutes to role-play the key point in the encounter between Ms. Reynolds and the staff member(s) as Ms. Reynolds seeks to resolve the supervisory issue. Each group will meet between sessions to work out the details for roles to be played and the general outline of the way the role-play will proceed. Group members should be prepared to present the rationale for their approach in the role-play to the larger group and to discuss the consequences and any unexpected events that may occur in the role-play.

POSSIBLE ROLES ASSUMED BY TASK GROUP MEMBERS:

⊙ Ms. Reynolds – Program Supervisor:

⊙ Ms. Alvarez – Casework Supervisor:

⊙ Ms. Bennett – Direct Service Worker:

⊙ Ms. Hernandez – Secretary:

⊙ Ms. Morse - Executive Director:

⊙ Program Supervisor – Administrative Group:

⊙ Program Participant:

⊙ Board Member:

ACTIVITY 4-11: Illustrating Gender Issues–*Soliloquy*

IN THE CLASSROOM: *Soliloquy* will help you to think about cultural perceptions of gender and their impact on practice.

IN THE FIELD: *Soliloquy* is a useful tool for raising awareness in a light way about the obvious and subtle ways assumptions and attitudes about gender and gender roles persist. The activity is suitable for use with older school-age children and youth through adults. You might also use it in workshops and in-service training to raise staff awareness about gender and gender roles. If *Carousel* is available on video and the group has access to a video player, cue the tape to the performance of *Soliloquy*, view the video, and proceed with the discussion. In groups where members may have hearing difficulties, use a transcript of the lyrics. If members have visual constraints, the audiotape is preferable to the video

MATERIALS: Tape recorder, tape; CD and CD player; or VCR, TV, and video of *Carousel* cued to appropriate section of the tape.

GROUP SIZE: 30

TIME REQUIRED: 15 minutes

SPACE REQUIREMENTS: A classroom that allows students to sit close enough to hear the recording or view the video easily.

PREPARATION: The instructor will assemble and check the equipment.

INSTRUCTIONS: Listen carefully to the song, noting assumptions the performer makes about gender roles and ways the music reinforces those views. Using your notes, participate in the discussion considering whether gender has as much power and influence over ways males and females are perceived today as in the past. Identify what has changed and what has stayed the same. Note any issues that are not addressed in the lyrics with respect to gender roles and speculate on the reasons for their absence. Also discuss to the potential impact assumptions and perceptions of gender and gender roles have in your practice situation.

PRACTITIONER'S NOTES:

· With what types of groups would you use this activity?

· At what stage(s) of group development would this activity be useful?

· How would member's characteristics, skills, and abilities influence the way you would modify and implement this activity?

· How would this activity contribute to the group goals, members' goals, and session goals?

· At what point in the group meeting would you introduce the activity?

· How would you evaluate the usefulness and impact of the activity on the group and its members?

Source: The soundtrack from *Carousel is* readily available from sources on the web (e.g., ProMusicFind.com) and may also be available in local library CD and tape collections.

ACTIVITY 4-12: Illustrating Perceptions of Urban Adolescent Boys–*Officer Krupke*

IN THE CLASSROOM: *Officer Krupke* will help you to explore some of society's perceptions of young, urban males living in poverty and the impact of those perceptions on practice.

IN THE FIELD: *Officer Krupke* raises the obvious and subtle ways assumptions and attitudes that adults may hold about young, urban males. The activity is suitable for use in groups of older school-age children and youth through adults where the facilitator wishes to introduce a discussion of gender and class stereotyping. *Officer Krupke* may also be used in workshops and in-service training to raise staff awareness about gender stereotyping and its subtle and not-so-subtle impact on practice. If *West Side Story* is available on video and the group has access to a video player, cue the tape to the performance of *Office Krupke*, view the video, and proceed with the discussion. In groups where members may have hearing difficulties, use a transcript of the lyrics. If members have visual constraints, the audiotape is clearly preferable to the video. Some of the slang used in the lyrics may need explanation. Be prepared to clarify unfamiliar terms.

MATERIALS: Tape recorder, tape; CD and CD player; or VCR, TV, and video of *West Side Story* cued to appropriate section of the tape.

GROUP SIZE: 30

TIME REQUIRED: 15 minutes

SPACE REQUIREMENTS: A classroom that allows students to sit close enough to hear the recording or view the video easily.

PREPARATION: Assemble and check the equipment. Prepare discussion questions.

INSTRUCTIONS: Listen intently to the song, noting the views various authorities have about young, urban males who live in New York's poorer neighborhoods. Think about how closely the views expressed in the song mirror views you may have heard in the past or in current situations. Explore whether these attitudes are dated or whether similar notions are present in today's culture. Give specific examples of similarities and differences. Consider the dynamics association with the intersection of gender, age, and class. Note any issues that are not addressed in the lyrics with respect to gender roles, class, and/or age, and speculate on the reasons for their absence. Conclude your discussion by exploring the potential impact assumptions and perceptions of gender and gender roles have in your practice situation.

PRACTITIONER'S NOTES:

· With what types of groups would you use this activity?

· At what stage(s) of group development would this activity be useful?

· How would member's characteristics, skills, and abilities influence the way you would modify and implement this activity?

·   How would this activity contribute to the group goals, members' goals, and session goals?

·   At what point in the group meeting would you introduce the activity?

·   How would you evaluate the usefulness and impact of the activity on the group and its members?

Source: The soundtrack from *West Side Story is* readily available from sources on the web (e.g., ProMusicFind.com) and may also be available in local library CD and tape collections.

ACTIVITY 4-13: Illustrating Perceptions of Women–
I'm Gonna Be an Engineer

IN THE CLASSROOM: *I'm Gonna Be an Engineer* raises the issue of women's roles and the impact of cultural restrictions on practice with women.

IN THE FIELD: *I'm Gonna Be An Engineer* is a useful tool to introduce discussion about the obvious and subtle ways attitudes about appropriate roles for women in the workplace. The activity is suitable for use with older school-age children and youth through adults to raise awareness and to challenge stereotypes. You may also use it for similar purposes in agency-based workshops and in-service training. If you are planning more than one session on this topic, you will find additional songs on the Web to amplify the discussion. (e.g., lyrics for *Independent Women* by Destiny's Child can be found at www.lyricsdomain.com/4/destinys_child/independent_women.html and The Fat Patrol's Greatest Hits–Songs to Celebrate Fat Women can be downloaded from www.largesse.net/Archives/songs.html). With any audio resource, use a transcript of the lyrics for members with hearing difficulties.

MATERIALS: Tape recorder, tape

GROUP SIZE: 30

TIME REQUIRED: 15 minutes

SPACE REQUIREMENTS: A classroom with seating for students close enough to hear the recording easily.

PREPARATION: The instructor will assemble and check the equipment.

INSTRUCTIONS: Listen closely to the song's lyrics, noting the views the woman has experienced in relation to key figures in her life. Use your notes to contribute to the discussion exploring current attitudes with respect to women's roles in the home and in the workplace. Give specific examples of similarities and differences. Note any issues that are not addressed in the lyrics with respect to gender roles, family relationships, workplace opportunities and attitudes. Consider the reasons for their absence. Also consider the potential impact assumptions and perceptions of women's roles have in your practice situation.

PRACTITIONER'S NOTES:

· With what types of groups would you use this activity?

· At what stage(s) of group development would this activity be useful?

· How would member's characteristics, skills, and abilities influence the way you would modify and implement this activity?

·   How would this activity contribute to the group goals, members' goals, and session goals?

·   At what point in the group meeting would you introduce the activity?

·   How would you evaluate the usefulness and impact of the activity on the group and its members?

Source: The recording is available on *Carry It On* by Pete Seeger, Jane Sapp, and Si Kahn, issued by Flying Fish Records and available from on-line booksellers (e.g., Barnes&Noble.com).

ACTIVITY 4-14: Developing Role-Play Scenarios

IN THE CLASSROOM: In this activity you will generate topics for discussion of issues in group supervision based on students' experiences.

IN THE FIELD: In groups that are experiencing problems with the group process, this activity might be used as a vehicle for you and the group members to raise those issues in a less direct and less threatening manner than through responses to questions that you might have raised with the group. You may also use this activity in groups where you and the group wish to increase members' input and responsibility for the work of the group.

MATERIALS: One *Report Back Form* per task group.

GROUP SIZE: 30

TIME REQUIRED: 30 minutes

SPACE REQUIREMENTS: A classroom with space for role-play "stage" area and seating for observers.

PREPARATION: The instructor will prepare the room to support the activity.

INSTRUCTIONS: Divide into task groups of six to seven students. Each task group will to select a note-taker who will record the short scenario developed by the group based on the assigned topic: Handling a problem in the supervision group's process. Each group will create a role-play that will run approximately 10 minutes. Each role-play supervision group will be composed of five staff members and will have a supervisor who will choose her/his leadership style in relation to the presenting scenario. In developing the scenario, you should include some details on the following areas [Note: The more realistic, the better the role-play will help to illustrate key issues in group supervision]:

1. The agency context;
2. The main issue facing the group and the supervisor;
3. The positions each of the five staff members hold in the agency; and
4. The roles each staff member typically plays in the group.

PRACTITIONER'S NOTES:

· With what types of groups would you use this activity?

· At what stage(s) of group development would this activity be useful?

· How would member's characteristics, skills, and abilities influence the way you would modify and implement this activity?

· How would this activity contribute to the group goals, members' goals, and session goals?

· At what point in the group meeting would you introduce the activity?

· How would you evaluate the usefulness and impact of the activity on the group and its members?

Source: Adapted with permission from *MODULE 2: GROUP SUPERVISION* of the Clinically Informed Supervision Seminar developed by the author in conjunction with The University of Maine School of Social Work.

ROLE-PLAY SCENARIO: Handling a Problem in the Supervision Group's Process

INSTRUCTIONS: In each task group, select a note taker who will record the short scenario developed by the group based on the assigned topic. Role-plays will run approximately 10 minutes. Each role-play supervision group will be composed of 5 staff members and will have a supervisor who will choose her/his leadership style in relation to the presenting scenario. In developing the scenario, the group should include some details on the following areas [the more realistic, the better the role-play will help illustrate key issues in group supervision]:

1. The agency context;
2. The main issue facing the group and the supervisor;
3. The positions each of the 5 staff members hold in the agency; and
4. The roles each staff member typically plays in the group.

REPORT BACK FORM: *Developing Role-play Scenarios*

TASK GROUP MEMBERS:

ROLE-PLAY SCENARIO: The beginning session in group supervision

1. The agency context:

2. The main issue facing the group and the supervisor:

3. Staff positions:

a.

b.

c.

d.

e. e.

4. Role typically played in group:

a.

b.

c.

d.

ACTIVITY 4-15: Evaluation of Practice

IN THE CLASSROOM: This activity will give you practice in applying content on evaluation of practice.

IN THE FIELD: You might use this activity in staff in-service training or in professional development workshops. You might also use it with program advisory boards or agency boards with responsibility for program oversight. You may choose to adapt the activity by asking members to submit practice situations to use in place of vignettes.

MATERIALS: Readings on evaluation of practice with groups [e.g., Toseland, R.W. and Rivas, R.F. (2001) *An introduction to group work practice (4ᵗʰ ed.).* Boston: Allyn & Bacon, Ch. 13], instruction sheets and vignettes.

GROUP SIZE: 30

TIME REQUIRED: 50 minutes.

SPACE REQUIREMENTS: Classroom with breakout areas for task group discussion.

PREPARATION: Complete the assigned reading before the session where the class will discuss methods of evaluation of practice. Review the instruction sheets and vignettes.

INSTRUCTIONS: Divide into six task groups. Select a vignette with which to work. Also select a recorder/reporter who will present the group's work in the discussion with the larger group. You will have 30 minutes to complete the activity. The instructor will be available for consultation during the activity. Move to your group's meeting location. At the 25-minute mark, your group should draw their discussion to a close. Reconvene as a class, and give report-back to the class when your group's turn comes. As each group makes its report, note links between the readings and the group reports

PRACTITIONER'S NOTES:

· With what types of groups would you use this activity?

· At what stage(s) of group development would this activity be useful?

· How would member's characteristics, skills, and abilities influence the way you would modify and implement this activity?

· How would this activity contribute to the group goals, members' goals, and session goals?

· At what point in the group meeting would you introduce the activity?

· How would you evaluate the usefulness and impact of the activity on the group and its members?

Vignette 1 – Teen Parent Program: You are the administrative team for a program for teenage parents. The program is funded by the federal government under a grant, which requires that 10% of the monies be devoted to evaluation. The program components include: (1) home visiting and individual casework support; (2) group services which concentrate on parenting skills; (3) referral for appropriate educational or job training services; (4) home day care services. Your task today is to develop evaluation procedures, which will document the effectiveness of the group services component. Be sure to consider the following issues:

- What information do you need to document that a service has taken place?
- How will line staff be involved in the development of the evaluation plan?
- What aspects of parenting skills will be taught?
- Which key variables will be used to document program effectiveness?
- What methods might be employed to test program effectiveness?

Vignette 2 – Settlement House Group Services: You are a supervisor team in charge of group services in a settlement house. Your staff includes 3 BSW workers who provide after-school recreational and social development services for neighborhood children ages 6-12. The settlement house is located in a section of Chicago which is economically, ethnically, and racially diverse. The population of children served reflects this diversity. At times, clashes between the children reflect the tensions in the community.

As supervisors, you are concerned that your staff provides a high quality of service to these children. The settlement house has not required any record keeping beyond attendance reports for each session. You feel that additional documentation of the services provided could improve staff interventions and provide the basis for in-service training. Consider some of the issues that are involved in instituting this new requirement:

- ⊙ How will you gain staff cooperation?
- ⊙ What type of recording will you ask staff to do?
- ⊙ How will you train staff in these new procedures?
- ⊙ What are three possible ways you might use these records?

Vignette 3 – Therapy Group: Your team is working with a group of students at a local city college. The group is designed for students who exhibit extreme anxiety about answering questions in class and about participating in class discussions. Devise an evaluation design that will track the effects of the group service for these individuals. Be sure to consider the following issues:

- ⊙ The severity of the behavior prior to participation in the group.
- ⊙ The key indicator(s) you will use to track the progress of group members.
- ⊙ The instrument you will use to track members' progress.
- ⊙ The method(s) you will use to document change.
- ⊙ How you will know when group members have reached their goals.

Chapter 5
Ending Activities with Groups in Generalist Practice

ENDING ACTIVITIES WITH GROUPS IN GENERALIST PRACTICE

In the *separation stage* the group's work is done and members begin to disengage from each other, from the worker, and from the group as a whole, making the transition to the next phase of their life experience. Group members and workers alike respond in a variety of ways, both productive and unproductive, to the ending of the group. In this stage of group development you may see the gamut of responses from a reappearance of earlier difficult behaviors to effective efforts to make the transition from the group to the next phase of growth and development. Garland, Jones, and Kolodny (1973) have identified some of these responses: denial, regression, flight, continuing need for the group, recapitulation of earlier phases of group development, and evaluation.

The activities in this chapter support positive ways of summing up of the group's experiences for the group as a whole and for individual members and seek to avoid those strategies that detract from a satisfactory ending of the group. Moreover, these activities help members make the transition from the group conscious and deliberate by helping them to look at what they have accomplished and how they will build on their accomplishments after they leave the group. These fourteen activities are ordered from the most complex, requiring considerable advance planning by both the instructor and class members, to those that can be accomplished with minimal preparation.

In the classroom as well as in staff training or in professional development workshops, the instructor may use these activities as simulations to enhance content students are studying about ways to assist a group through the separation stage. Your class may also use them as actual means of drawing your class as a socio-educational group to a close. For example, in A 5-1 *Group Life – A Photo Essay* you will work with a task group over a substantial portion of the semester, recording the activities that you have worked on together and documenting key events in your group's experiences. The end result will be a photographic essay that is retrospective as you look back over your work together and prospective as you look to the future building on those experiences. Each of these fourteen activities focuses you and the class on a look back at what has been accomplished and encourages you to envision the next steps in your journey toward your goal as a professional social worker.

In A 5-3 *Endings* the class takes the primary responsibility for the closing session of the group, with task groups creating and implementing activities that reflect the experiences in task groups and in class, summarize class, group, and individual accomplishments, and look to the future beyond the group. In the remaining activities, the instructor is responsible for the preparation and organization; the class members implement the activity, using creativity and imagination in summing up the group's work together and saying good-bye to individual members and the class as a whole. To highlight the parallel process of your experiences as a member of a group in the academic setting with those of group members in the social service agencies, each activity includes suggestions for application in the professional practice setting. You will also find approaches for adapting the activities for diverse populations.

Activities A 5-8 *Leaving My Mark* and A 5-10 *Branching Out* reflect additional dimensions of the separation phase. *Leaving My Mark* honors what you each have brought to the class experience. The markers left at the school are tangible reminders symbolizing those contributions. *Branching Out* is a visual metaphor for the transition you are about to make. The resulting mobile of branches and leaves is a reminder of class member's connections with each other, with the branches pointing in the different directions members will take as they leave the class. Activity A 5-2 *Growth Pots* further elaborates the theme of individual growth grounded in socio-educational encounters, using an arts and crafts approach to making this theme visible.

Two activities, A 5-6 *Closing Group Collage* and A 5-7 *The Group Web*, use a collaborative arts and crafts approach to facilitating ways for class members to draw their work to a close. In four activities, A 5-4 *Group Poem*, A 5-5 *Memory Book*, A 5-11 *Mirror, Mirror*, and A 5-13 *Recapitulating the Group Timeline* writing is the primary means for class members to sum up their experience with the group. Activity A 5-12 *Semester Review* the instructor takes primary responsibility for the activity and uses creative visualization to help class members recall salient events in the class history.

Activities A 5-9 *Famous Last Words* and A 5-14 *Parting Gifts* concentrate on the interpersonal aspects of the separation stage by giving and receiving gifts that symbolize significant aspects of the separation from the class and the transition to the next phase of students' lives. In *Parting Gifts* class members select small, inexpensive gifts as metaphors for good wishes for each other as you leave this class and start on new endeavors. *Famous Last Words* gives you a way to sum up your experience with each other and to wish each other well.

As in earlier chapters, remember to use the Practitioner's Notes to make your final observations about the activities you have experienced, noting ways that you can begin to use them in your practice. I hope these activities and the notes you have made on each of them will serve as a springboard for new creative approaches to working with groups.

References:

Garland, J.A., Jones, H.E., Kolodny, R.L. (1973). A model for stages of group development in social work groups (pp. 17-71). In S. Bernstein (Ed.). *Explorations in group work: Essays in theory and practice (Reprint)*. Bloomfield, CT: Practitioner's Press.

ACTIVITY 5-1: Group Life – A Photo Essay on the Life of a Student Task Group

IN THE CLASSROOM: In this activity you and your task group will use photography to document task group behavior at particular stages of group development. You will have an opportunity to experience an alternative form of communication in the final phase of the activity when the task group will present its photo essay in the last class session of the semester.

IN THE FIELD: This activity is suitable for use with a broad range of groups, school children through adults. For example, it has been used with children and youth in the Lynn Public Schools to begin to use photography as a way to record their impressions of life in Lynn and in therapeutic work with teens to record family life experiences. How might you use photography as an intervention with your groups in field or in your later practice?

When you use this activity in the agency, you will need signed permission and release forms from the group members or from the parents or guardians for any groups of children or teens. You should discuss the purpose(s) of the activity, guidelines for the project, and confidentiality with the group members and/or parents before you implement the activity. For groups where expense might prohibit the activity, a range of funding sources should be explored (e.g., agency funding, sponsorship by a local camera club, grant writing to local businesses or family foundations).

MATERIALS: Student groups are responsible for providing the materials and equipment for this project, including: one camera per group (disposable cameras will work as long as students purchase models for indoor and outdoor photography), film, the developed photographs, poster board, other art supplies students choose to use.

GROUP SIZE: 30 maximum

TIME REQUIRED: Student groups' preparation time outside class: one day to take the photographs; time for developing the prints (varies depending on available photo processing outlets); time to prepare photo poster presentation. In class time: 10 minutes for poster presentation.

SPACE REQUIREMENTS: Wall space to accommodate posters.

PREPARATION: *Early in the semester:* Review the instruction sheet, asking any questions or points for clarification that will help you understand the purpose of the activity and the goal for the project. Meet with your group to plan how you will document the stages of group development that your group will encounter. Assemble the equipment—one camera per group (disposable cameras will work, as long they are models for indoor and outdoor photography), film, the developed photographs, poster board, other art supplies the group chooses to use. Students who agree to be photographed should complete a standard Photo Release form. Check with the instructor for samples of standard Release forms.

Agree on a meeting time to take the photographs. Photos should convey the essence of the way your task group functions and any other key point about the group that you want to communicate to the viewer. Once the photo shoot is accomplished, have the photos developed in whatever size and format suits the plan for the poster. When the photos are ready, meet to prepare the poster. Be prepared to discuss the poster at the viewing at the Poster Session.

The instructor will be available for consultation on the project either by phone, email, or appointment outside of class. Please have specific questions or points to raise for discussion to make the best use of the consultation.

INSTRUCTIONS: *The Poster Session:* Arrange your group's poster on the wall or in the designated space in the classroom. The class will take 5-10 minutes to view the posters and then will be seated. Each group in turn will discuss their poster, answering any questions that may arise from the class. As a class, decide where the posters will be displayed, if everyone agrees on sharing their work with the larger school community.

PRACTITIONER'S NOTES:

- At what stage(s) of group development would this activity be useful?

- How would member's characteristics, skills, and abilities influence the way you would modify and implement this activity?

- How would this activity contribute to the group goals, members' goals, and session goals?

- At what point in the group meeting would you introduce the activity?

- How would you evaluate the usefulness and impact of the activity on the group and its members?

Source: From a personal communication with David Parsons, Photographer, Lynn, MA. Adapted by permission.

ACTIVITY 5-2: Growth Pots

IN THE CLASSROOM: Creating a *Growth Pot* will give you a visual metaphor for your goals for continuing professional growth. The seeds that you choose to plant in the completed pot will extend the metaphor.

IN THE FIELD: You can use this activity in the separation stage with the pots as an object that the members can take with them as a remembrance of the group experience. In preparing for this activity you should make a sample pot so that you can spot areas where group members might have difficulty and develop a way to address the potential problems. For example, to eliminate messiness in transferring the potting soil, you might fill small plastic bags with the right amount for the pots. You could also make separate seed packets for each member by sealing 3-4 seeds in small envelopes. For younger groups, choose large seeds that are easier to manage (e.g., beans). Group members can plant the pots once they have dried.

The activity can be used with young children who have sufficient eye-hand coordination or they can make the pots with adult assistance. In groups where some members may need particular accommodations, forming pairs that can work together to create their pots encourages cooperation and support in completing the project. The activity may be contraindicated for groups with low impulse control, given the potential for breakage and other damage. Consider the range of groups with whom you might use this activity and those with whom you would not use it.

MATERIALS: 6" clay pots, Modge Podge, 12-15 foam brushes, newspaper or plastic sheeting to protect tables, 12-15 scissors, magazines with relevant social work content (e.g., *Social Work Today,* news magazines), plastic or other non-stick surface for drying the pots, seeds for easy-to-grow plants (e.g., Kentucky Wonder Beans, morning glories, marigolds), potting soil, broom and dustpan or vacuum to clean floor when project is completed.

GROUP SIZE: 30 maximum

TIME REQUIRED: 20-30 minutes.

SPACE REQUIREMENTS: A classroom with table space to accommodate the project.

PREPARATION: The instructor and the class members will decide how the materials will be obtained (e.g., donations to the instructor to purchase supplies, volunteers to bring in certain items). The instructor will make a sample collage pot, noting potential problem areas in the process.

INSTRUCTIONS: The class will do this activity six to eight weeks before the end of the semester. To begin the activity, you will choose pictures and printed words from the magazines to be glued to the outside of the pots. As you look at the available materials, you should consider ways that the pot will be a metaphor for your professional growth. Once you have enough pictures/words to cover the pots, you can apply the Modge Podge to your pot, inside and out. Next you will apply the pictures and words, covering the pot in a patchwork, making sure all the items are coated on the outside with Modge Podge. Place your finished pot on plastic or other non-stick material for the drying process.

At the close of the session, collect your potting soil packets and seeds. You will plant the seeds before the next session, watering the pots according to the plant growing instructions for the seeds selected. The instructor will check with the class on the growth process periodically, asking you to relate stories of both success and mishaps that will occur and to encourage you to draw analogies with the process of professional growth. On the last day of class, the class members will bring their Growth Pots to class and use them to illustrate their growth and development over the semester.

PRACTITIONER'S NOTES:

- At what stage(s) of group development would this activity be useful?

- How would member's characteristics, skills, and abilities influence the way you would modify and implement this activity?

- How would this activity contribute to the group goals, members' goals, and session goals?

- At what point in the group meeting would you introduce the activity?

- How would you evaluate the usefulness and impact of the activity on the group and its members?

Source: Based on an activity developed by Elin MacKinnon, LCSW. Used with permission.

ACTIVITY 5-3: Endings

IN THE CLASSROOM: This activity will assist the class in reflecting on accomplishments you have made in the class and/or in your semester-long small task group. Group members will develop a series of activities to draw the semester's experiences to a close.

IN THE FIELD: You may choose to use *Endings* in your practice with groups of older grade school children through adults, making adjustments for developmental level and setting. Depending on the age and the accomplishments of the group, you may decide to assign responsibilities for the closing session. In either case, if the small groups choose not to report back, you should discuss the activity with them at the end of the planning session to insure that the final session runs smoothly.

MATERIALS: None, except for items the task groups need for each activity.

GROUP SIZE: 30 maximum

TIME REQUIRED: Two class sessions: Session 1 requires 10 minutes to review the initial instructions and 40 minutes for planning; Session 2 requires a minimum of 45 minutes for final meeting activities.

SPACE REQUIREMENTS: A classroom plus space for breakout sections.

INSTRUCTIONS: In your task group, review the key points in the history of the class and/or your small group activities. Your final task is to plan the closing session. The last class will consist of a series of activities developed by these small task groups. Your group may choose to do an activity that will help the class to reflect on accomplishments verbally or primarily non-verbally (e.g., an artistic or drama activity). Depending on the time allotted for class, each group's activity will be time limited. For example, a 50-minute class session would limit each activity to a maximum of five to six minutes each, taking into account the time needed to move from one activity to another.

The planning session: Divide into your task groups. These groups will be based on task groups that have worked together over a period of time, or they may be created for this activity through a mutually agreeable method of group formation. Each group will choose one aspect of the closing session (e.g., opening the session, reflecting on group challenges, summarizing group accomplishments, celebrating change/progress, saying good-bye, looking to the future). Your task group will review key experiences in the life of the group (i.e., either for the class or the on-going task group, if one has existed) and the significant accomplishments of the group. Based on your chosen aspect, the task group will develop an activity. Your group will decide whether to report your plan to the class and elicit whatever cooperation you may need from the class members for the closing session or keep the activity as a surprise for the closing session. If you choose not to report to the class, you will meet briefly with the instructor after class to get approval for your plans. If you have questions and find areas of the instructions that may need further discussion, consult with your instructor.

The closing session: In the closing session your group will implement your activity and will participate in the activities designed by the other groups. You may wish to take notes on the activities each group presents for future use in your practice with groups.

PRACTITIONER'S NOTES:

· With what types of groups would you use this activity?

· At what stage(s) of group development would this activity be useful?

· How would member's characteristics, skills, and abilities influence the way you would modify and implement this activity?

· How would this activity contribute to the group goals, members' goals, and session goals?

· At what point in the group meeting would you introduce the activity?

· How would you evaluate the usefulness and impact of the activity on the group and its members?

ACTIVITY 5-4: Group Poem

IN THE CLASSROOM: The *Group Poem* offers the class a creative way to articulate the issues involved in drawing the semester's experience to a close.

IN THE FIELD: The *Group Poem* works well with older children, teens, and adults. You can use it in the separation phase to conclude the group. You can also use it in the intimacy phase of group development to promote group cohesion and a sense of working together. This activity requires a basic level of writing skill and some creativity with words. The discussion of the forms poetry suggested later in these instructions might jumpstart the activity for those who may be less confident of their creative writing ability.

MATERIALS: A legal sized pad of paper and enough pens/pencils for the class members; duplicating facilities to make copies of the completed poem for each class member.

GROUP SIZE: 10-15, ideally; can be done with 30 maximum.

TIME REQUIRED: 30-40 minutes, depending on group size.

SPACE REQUIREMENTS: Enough space for students to be seated comfortably for writing.

PREPARATION: The instructor will assemble the materials.

INSTRUCTIONS: The class will complete this activity two weeks before the end of the semester. The instructor may ask you to give some examples of the styles of poetry with which you are familiar. Decide which ones are relevant to the class as it draws to a close. As you think about what has happened during the semester in this class, jot down some ideas for a first sentence for a group poem. When the instructor asks for a first line, you may choose to read what you have written. The class will select a first line from those offered. The author of the line selected will write that line on the pad of paper. Then another class member will suggest the next line and write it below the first line on the pad. The pad is passed from person to person, each one adding a line. When the poem is completed, a volunteer can read it to the group. The instructor will ask for a volunteer to type the poem and forward it to the class—preferably by email. If email is not available, the instructor will be responsible for duplicating the poem and distributing copies to class members in the last session.

PRACTITIONER'S NOTES:

·   At what stage(s) of group development would this activity be useful?

·   How would member's characteristics, skills, and abilities influence the way you would modify and implement this activity?

·   How would this activity contribute to the group goals, members' goals, and session goals?

· At what point in the group meeting would you introduce the activity?

· How would you evaluate the usefulness and impact of the activity on the group and its members?

Source: Contributed by Marcia B. Cohen, PhD, Professor, University of New England School of Social Work, Portland, ME.

ACTIVITY 5-5: Memory Books

IN THE CLASSROOM: In this activity, you will contribute tangible items that represent key classroom experiences (e.g., the list of class norms, the title of a key assignment with a few sentences summarizing its significance in the class experience, or a photo of the class taken at some point during the semester). The items will be compiled into a Memory Book that will represent the class's accomplishments over the semester.

IN THE FIELD: Similarly, in your practice with groups you can use this activity to give group members a tangible reminder of the group's achievements. Using the Practitioner's Notes, explore ways of incorporating this activity into your work with groups in the practice setting.

MATRIALS: Copier-ready items created during the semester that have particular significance for class members, task groups, or the class as a whole; materials to create the books (e.g., heavy construction paper for covers, staple, staples).

GROUP SIZE: 30-40

TIME REQUIRED: Preparation time outside class to choose the items for the Memory Book and to assemble the book; 45 minutes to discuss the submitted items, select the cover design, and select volunteers to do the organization, duplicating, and assembling of the copies for the class; time to duplicate copies outside of class time.

SPACE REQUIREMENTS: Classroom plus breakout areas for small task groups.

PREPARATION: Individually and in your task groups, if you have been meeting with them over the semester, select a maximum of one item for yourself and, with your group, one item relevant to the group experience. Be prepared to tell the class why you have chosen these items during the discussion portion of the activity. The class will also need a design for the cover of the Memory Book. You may submit a design you have created, or you might collaborate with class members to create a design.

INSTRUCTIONS: Bring the items and the cover design, if you have made one, to the class session where you will assemble the Memory Book. During the discussion, relate your reason(s) for submitting the items you and your group have chosen. As a class, decide the layout for each page and the order in which the items will appear in the memory book. The class will also select a design for the cover either by choosing one from those submitted or asking the cover designers to collaborate on merging selected elements from the designs submitted. A group of volunteers will assemble the Memory Book for the final class and will be responsible for duplicating enough copies for the class and the instructor. If your School of Social Work keeps documents for the School's archives, you might give a copy to the School as well. Distribute the copies at the last session.

PRACTITIONER'S NOTES:

·   At what stage(s) of group development would this activity be useful?

·   How would member's characteristics, skills, and abilities influence the way you would modify and implement this activity?

· How would this activity contribute to the group goals, members' goals, and session goals?

· At what point in the group meeting would you introduce the activity?

· How would you evaluate the usefulness and impact of the activity on the group and its members?

ACTIVITY 5-6: Closing Group Collage

IN THE CLASSROOM: The *Closing Group Collage* gives you an opportunity to sum up what you have learned and to contribute your observations about the key events in the classroom experience through an artistic medium.

IN THE FIELD: You can use this activity in the separation stage to help group members give form and substance to their thoughts and feelings about ending the group. This craft activity can help you to give focus to the ensuing discussion, encourage members to talk about the ending of the group, and to realize they are not alone in their feelings or experiences. Some group members may object to tearing rather than cutting the paper. Where the goal of the activity is to use the media as a way to express feeling, the torn paper method provides a more immediate connection with the materials than interposing a tool (scissors) between the individual and the materials. However, depending on group members' characteristics and the specific goals of the activity, group members may use scissors rather than the torn paper method if feelings are not the primary focus of the activity. Glue sticks may work better for some groups and in some settings, limiting the messiness involved in using other types of glue or paste. Whatever the setting, everyone needs to be careful not to damage surfaces or leave debris in the room after the activity. If other groups use the room, the collages should be removed at the end of the session and stored in the instructor's office or taken home by group members.

MATERIALS: Glue or paste; construction paper or poster board; other items suitable for gluing to construction paper or art boards (e.g., magazine pictures, words, buttons, beads, feathers, leaves, small shells, pebbles and/or other "found natural materials, items created in the course of class activities); large sheet of paper to combine group collages into a class collage, tape or other means of attaching the combined collage to the wall.

GROUP SIZE: 30

TIME REQUIRED: 30-45 minutes, depending on follow-up discussion

SPACE REQUIREMENTS: Sufficient surfaces (e.g., tables, drawing boards, floor) to create the collages in small task groups and wall space to display the finished class project.

PREPARATION: Either the instructor can assemble the materials or request the class to bring in materials for this activity. In either case, the instructor should make a sample collage to determine the pitfalls in the activity and find ways to remedy any problems that arise. The instructor should tape a large sheet of paper on the wall for assembling the group collages into a class collage before the activity begins.

INSTRUCTIONS: Listen carefully to the directions the instructor gives for completing the activity. Raise any questions you may have about the procedure. Divide into task groups of five to six members. Choose a reporter who will describe the group's collage to the class when it reconvenes. Select the materials you will use for your collage. You may then begin the activity by choosing a background sheet to form the base for your contribution to the group collage. Using a torn-paper method, you will tear shapes in colors that symbolize your particular views, feelings, and/or experiences during the semester in this class. Glue the shapes and other items, if the project includes them, on the background sheet. Work with the other members of your group to assemble your individual contributions into the group's collage. When the class reconvenes, your group will post the collage on the sheet taped to the wall, considering its relation to the other group's collages, thus indicating their view of their relationship to the class as a whole. When the class collage is assembled, each group will describe what their collage symbolizes and participate in a discussion reflecting on the meaning of the semester's experiences.

PRACTITIONER'S NOTES:

·   At what stage(s) of group development would this activity be useful?

·   How would member's characteristics, skills, and abilities influence the way you would modify and implement this activity?

·   How would this activity contribute to the group goals, members' goals, and session goals?

·   At what point in the group meeting would you introduce the activity?

·   How would you evaluate the usefulness and impact of the activity on the group and its members?

ACTIVITY 5-7: The Group Web

IN THE CLASSROOM: The *Group Web* is a highly interactive activity in which you and the other group members will use colored yarn to create a web, interweaving it with items that symbolize important aspects of the group's experience. This activity offers you a chance to recapitulate key events in the life of the group and represent those events visually and artistically.

IN THE FIELD: With suitable variations and safeguards, you can use *The Group Web* with almost anyone that has sufficient memory, verbal ability, and dexterity to do the weaving and select the objects to symbolize the class's experiences. You can substitute a frame made of supple twigs or use a large hoop for the foam board/pin loom. Plastic frames (e.g., a hula hoop) are harder to use because the yarn slips when objects are added. You will need to experiment to find a way to anchor the yarn securely. You can suspend completed webs as mobiles.

Students in one generalist practice class developed another variation on *The Group Web* called the Web of Change (SWK 462, Practice II, University of Maine School of Social Work, Fall 2003). Class members formed a large circle. The student starting the web held the ball of yarn while she told the class her most significant way she or her task group had changed during the semester. Holding one end of the yarn, she called another student's name and tossed the ball to her. The second student caught the ball and stated his most significant change. Holding on to the strand of yarn, he tossed the ball to the next student. The web grew more and more complex until all students had participated and were connected to the web.

MATERIALS: Yarn, long pushpins or t-pins to make the points for weaving, foam board as the loom base, scissors, a collection of symbolic items contributed by class members, markers.

GROUP SIZE: Small groups of 5-6 students or the whole class

TIME REQUIRED: 30 minutes to create the web; 5 minutes to view the finished product, 15 minutes to discuss the activity and its meaning for the group and/or class.

SPACE REQUIREMENTS: Enough table and wall space to accommodate the students doing the weaving and to display the finished product(s).

PREPARATION: Before the session where you will make *The Group Web*, you will think about the experiences you and the group have shared. You will select some objects that could be attached or inserted in the weaving that will symbolize key events you want to include. Bring those objects to the class session.

INSTRUCTIONS: As a group, select a foam board and box of pins. Create the loom for the weaving by affixing the pins to the foam board. Designs will vary by group. Make sure you have enough points around the perimeter so that each member of the group can attach their yarn to four or more points to form the warp or the basis for the web. You might want to use the number of points and the placement of your yarn to indicate something about your experience as a group member. Once everyone's yarn is attached, group members can fill in the design attaching the objects they have brought to add to the web. You may also wish to write or draw something on cardboard tags and attach the tags at various points on the web. If the group wishes, you can give the final design a title that sums up the essence of your group experience.

PRACTITIONER'S NOTES:

·   At what stage(s) of group development would this activity be useful?

·   How would member's characteristics, skills, and abilities influence the way you would modify and implement this activity?

·   How would this activity contribute to the group goals, members' goals, and session goals?

·   At what point in the group meeting would you introduce the activity?

·   How would you evaluate the usefulness and impact of the activity on the group and its members?

ACTIVITY 5-8: Leaving My Mark

IN THE CLASSROOM: *Leaving My Mark* will assist you and your classmates to draw the class to a close and to leave a tangible marker of the class's experience at the school.

IN THE FIELD: This activity is a suitable activity for any age group. For very young children not yet able to write their names on the rocks or members for whom small muscle control is difficult, you can write their names on the rocks they select. You may choose to eliminate the name writing component, asking group members to choose or bring a special natural element to leave in the garden. For example, shells, driftwood, and/or beach glass might be substituted in locations near water. Depending on the group's situation, you can either collect the rocks and the permanent markers before the last session or ask members each to bring a rock to the final session. If using the latter method, you may want to have a few extra rocks for those who may forget. Note that in groups with low impulse control, the facilitator may want to find a substitute for rocks and stones that can cause injury if thrown.

MATERIALS: A small collection of rocks (3-4" across) with a flat surface, permanent magic markers, and an area suitable for displaying the decorated rocks.

GROUP SIZE: 10-15

TIME REQUIRED: 15 minutes.

SPACE REQUIREMENTS: Table space for decorating the rocks plus an outdoor or indoor garden area for placing the rocks artistically.

PREPARATION: On the last day of class you will bring in a small rock, 3-4" across, with a flat surface. The instructor will supply permanent magic markers, an area suitable for displaying the decorated rocks—an outdoor garden space or an indoor collection of potted plants works well.

INSTRUCTIONS: Select a marker and decorate your rock with your name and other designs. Assemble at the garden location and choose a spot in the garden to place your rock.

PRACTITIONER'S NOTES:

- With what types of groups would you use this activity?

- At what stage(s) of group development would this activity be useful?

- How would member's characteristics, skills, and abilities influence the way you would modify and implement this activity?

·   How would this activity contribute to the group goals, members' goals, and session goals?

·   At what point in the group meeting would you introduce the activity?

·   How would you evaluate the usefulness and impact of the activity on the group and its members?

ACTIVITY 5-9: Famous Last Words

IN THE CLASSROOM: This activity will help you and the class acknowledge and explore the issues inherent in the separation phase of group development.

IN THE FIELD: *Famous Last Words* can be used as a closing exercise in groups in which the members' writing skills are equal to the activity. You might also use it as a way to stimulate interaction at other stages of group development. For example, at any stage of group development, you might ask the members to write a word, phrase, or sentence summarizing their thoughts, feelings, and/or reactions to the session. In this instance, the commentary should not be limited to positive statements. You can use the aggregate reactions to start the next session as a review or to raise issues needing discussion. For groups where writing is contraindicated, you could substitute drawing a picture or selecting a picture from magazines to tape or glue on the paper, resulting in a colorful collage.

You can vary the approach by having members sum up their responses to the group as a whole rather than to individual members. You would attach a large sheet of paper to the wall, making sure that the markers will not bleed through the paper onto the wall. You or a volunteer from the group would write the group name or designation in large, colorful letters in the center of the sheet (e.g., ***THE AFTERSCHOOL PROGRAM***). Members would each write a word or short statement that characterizes their experience with the class. In the separation phase when the group has had a stormy history or if members of subgroups have had a difficult experience in the group, the emphasis on positive statements may need extra reinforcement or the activity as a whole may be contraindicated.

MATERIALS: Assorted colorful copier paper, one sheet per class member, markers.

GROUP SIZE: 30 maximum

TIME REQUIRED: 15 – 20 minutes, depending on group size

SPACE REQUIREMENTS: Desk or table space for students to write notes with some degree of privacy.

PREPARATION: Collect the supplies needed for the activity.

INSTRUCTIONS: Spend a few minutes thinking about a positive statement you might make to each member of the class in parting. Select a sheet of colored copier paper and a marker. Write your name in the center of your paper. Pass the paper to the next person who will write a final message to you. Continue passing the papers around the circle until each person has a message from everyone in the group.

PRACTITIONER'S NOTES:

·   With what types of groups would you use this activity?

·   At what stage(s) of group development would this activity be useful?

·   How would member's characteristics, skills, and abilities influence the way you would modify and implement this activity?

·   How would this activity contribute to the group goals, members' goals, and session goals?

·   At what point in the group meeting would you introduce the activity?

·   How would you evaluate the usefulness and impact of the activity on the group and its members?

ACTIVITY 5-10: Branching Out

IN THE CLASSROOM: This activity is designed to help you and the class to draw your activities to a close and to help class members to focus on the transition process.

IN THE FIELD: *Branching Out* is a suitable separation activity for school age children through adults. Younger children can do leaf rubbings with adult supervision. Before you do the activity with the group, use the instructions below to make a partially completed sample to show the group. If the group is ending during autumn in an area where the leaves turn bright colors, you could assemble a collection of small, colorful leaves. You could supply slips of paper cut in strips 3" by 3/4" and ask each member to sign a slip. Group members would then select a leaf and place the leaf and their name between two pieces of waxed paper cut in circles, triangles, or ovals. In turn, using a warm iron, they would iron around the edges of the waxed paper, sealing in their leaf and their name. With younger groups, you would be responsible for doing the ironing. The finished products can be suspended or taped to a window, making an autumn stained glass farewell collage. If space permits, you can suspend a bare tree branch in the room or fix it firmly in a terra cotta pot using stones and florist's clay to weight the branch and pot. Choose a pot large enough to keep the branch securely anchored and a branch that is symmetrical to avoid it tipping over. Locate the pot and branch in a corner out of the room's traffic flow. Group members attach their leaves to the tree branches to form a group mobile.

MATERIALS: A tree branch or a large sheet of butcher paper with the outline of a many-branched tree drawn to fill most of the sheet, an assortment of large leaves freshly gathered, flat crayons or unwrapped stick crayons, copier paper and sheet of clean scrap paper – one per class member, reinforcements, fish line, scissors, tape.

GROUP SIZE: 5-30

TIME REQUIRED: 15-20 minutes.

SPACE REQUIREMENTS: Sufficient accessible wall space to attach the sheet with the tree or floor space to locate the branch in a pot, table space for class members to complete a leaf rubbing.

PREPARATION: Close to the time when the activity will be done, you will collect a small assortment of large leaves from trees and plants. Transport the leaves to class in a flat container to assure they remain unrumpled.

INSTRUCTIONS: Assist the instructor in posting the tree outline or suspending a bare tree branch in the room. If you are using an actual branch, be sure to fix it firmly in a terra cotta pot using stones and florist's clay to weight the branch and pot, making sure that it is balanced to avoid tipping over. At your workspace, select a leaf and place it on clean sheet of scrap paper. Cover the leaf with a sheet of white or light colored copier paper and hold it sandwiched securely between the two sheets. Rub an unwrapped crayon held with the broadest side against the paper over the leaf until the outline of the leaf appears. Personalize your leaf rubbing with your name and any positive parting message you want to share with the class. Cut out the leaf, punch a hole at the stem end, and place a reinforcement around the hole. Carefully thread a six-inch length of fish line through the hole. Hang your leaf rubbings from the branch to form a group mobile. As the activity proceeds, consider metaphors the leaves and branches suggest to you.

PRACTITIONER'S NOTES:

· With what types of groups would you use this activity?

· At what stage(s) of group development would this activity be useful?

· How would member's characteristics, skills, and abilities influence the way you would modify and implement this activity?

ACTIVITY 5-11: Mirror, Mirror

IN THE CLASSROOM: *Mirror, Mirror* offers you an opportunity to reflect on your growth as a social work student, on your purposeful use of roles that contributed to or detracted from achieving both your purpose and the purpose of the educational program. In this activity you will identify changes in your work from the beginning of the class through the final weeks of the course and link those changes to your professional foundation in social work knowledge, values, and skills. You will also consider the growth and change you have seen among the members of your ongoing task group and/or the class, providing each other with a mirror on your individual growth and evolution of the class.

IN THE FIELD: *Mirror, Mirror* is a useful ending activity with groups that have been focused on skill building, personal growth and development, and/or therapeutic interventions. It promotes insight into personal change and helps group members identify, acknowledge, and articulate the importance of those changes to each other. If the group has had a particularly difficult time working together at any point over the semester, you need to remember to keep the focus on the activity positive. It is important to avoid recapitulating those problem areas at a time when the group will have little opportunity to work through re-visited difficulties.

MATERIALS: Cardboard cutouts of mirrors, one per student. The mirrors should be large enough to allow students to write key words identifying areas of growth and change. Blue pens for printing and markers for decorating the mirrors and adding/underlining key words to classmates' mirrors.

GROUP SIZE: 15-20

TIME REQUIRED: 15 minutes to reflect and write key words on the mirror; 30 minutes to share reflections with the small group.

SPACE REQUIREMENTS: Enough space at desks or tables to complete the writing aspect of the activity, plus breakout areas for small groups to meet for the closing discussion if those have been part of the class experience.

INSTRUCTIONS: When you have received a mirror, use the blue pen to write the key words that indicate the positive growth and change you have seen in yourself over the semester. Write your name prominently either in the mirror's frame or on the back. Use the markers to decorate the mirror around the edges and on the back. When everyone has finished writing the key words and decorating the mirror, pass your mirror to the next member of the group. Each group member will use a marker either to add additional key words in colors other than blue, reflecting their perceptions of the mirror owner's positive growth and change or underline key words already written to indicate agreement with the mirror owner's perceptions. When everyone has written something on each mirror, retrieve your mirror and read what has been written. If time permits, you may have a discussion about your reactions to what is written on the mirrors. What words or reinforcement surprises you? What needs clarification?

PRACTITIONER'S NOTES:

· At what stage(s) of group development would this activity be useful?

·   How would member's characteristics, skills, and abilities influence the way you would modify and implement this activity?

·   How would this activity contribute to the group goals, members' goals, and session goals?

·   At what point in the group meeting would you introduce the activity?

·   How would you evaluate the usefulness and impact of the activity on the group and its members?

ACTIVITY 5-12: Semester Review—Creative Visualization

IN THE CLASSROOM: Doing a *Semester Review* using creative visualization will help you think back over the semester and gain a sense of what you and the class has accomplished during this time period. It will be a good preparation for the final activities in your task groups, if that has been part of the class experience, and with the class as a whole. This activity requires quiet concentration.

IN THE FIELD: You can use visualization activities with older children through adults to help the group regain a sense of what has gone before either in the life of the group or in their own lives. This activity can be used in both treatment and task groups. For example, a social worker used creative visualization as part of the in-service training for a group of women who had volunteered to be mentors for a group of teenage mothers. Each of the women had been a teenage mother herself. The worker introduced the activity as a way for the group members to remember what it had been like when they were going through the experiences that many of the girls were now having. She asked the group to sit quietly in a circle while she helped them to revisit that time in their lives. Some chose to close their eyes. The worker asked them to think back to the year of their pregnancy, to remember what it was like to be that age before they learned they were pregnant. Then she took them through the various experiences that teens faced with an unplanned pregnancy. From telling family and friends through to the delivery and birth. The women reported that the visualization helped them remember what those days had been like and made them more sensitive and less impatient with the teens with whom they were working.

When you use this activity in practice, you will need to consider carefully whether sufficient trust and communication is present in the group and between you and the group for the activity to be a valuable experience for group members. You will need to be well acquainted with the group members, their past history, and be careful in selecting words and phrases to raise issues with which the group is ready to address.

MATERIALS: None

GROUP SIZE: 10-30

TIME REQUIRED: 20 minutes

SPACE REQUIREMENTS: Space for class members to sit in a circle.

PREPARATION: Before the class where the activity will occur, the instructor should review the syllabus to select key points in this semester's class to use as phrases to guide class members recapitulation of the semester's events.

INSTRUCTIONS: Take your seat in the circle and prepare to listen quietly to the instructor's review of the semester. Closing your eyes may help you concentrate more fully on the instructor's words and on your memories of those points during the semester. As you listen to what the instructor says, visualize what was happening for you at that time—the events and the accompanying thoughts, feelings, and behavior that you experiences and that you saw around you. When the instructor completes the semester review, you should stay seated quietly a few moments and wait for instructions about the next closing activity.

PRACTITIONER'S NOTES:

- At what stage(s) of group development would this activity be useful?

- How would member's characteristics, skills, and abilities influence the way you would modify and implement this activity?

- How would this activity contribute to the group goals, members' goals, and session goals?

- At what point in the group meeting would you introduce the activity?

- How would you evaluate the usefulness and impact of the activity on the group and its members?

ACTIVITY 5-13: Recapitulating the Group's Timeline

IN THE CLASSROOM: This activity will help you to reflect on and visualize the stages of group development, identifying the stages through which your task group has passed.

IN THE FIELD: Group timelines are useful in the separation stage of group development to help the group visualize their accomplishments together and to recapitulate the stages as the group draws to a close. Groups may choose to embellish the timelines with items (e.g., photos, magazine illustrations, other artifacts that have meaning for the group) relevant to the stages of group development depicted. Other media may also be used to create the timeline. For example, if Power Point or a similar computer program is available, the group can create the timeline in successive slides.

MATERIALS: Paper, markers, masking tape, logs that students have kept for each meeting over the semester.

GROUP SIZE: 30-40

TIME REQUIRED: 30 minutes

SPACE REQUIREMENTS: Classroom, plus breakout areas for small groups.

PREPARATION: The instructor will assemble the materials. You will bring your class notes to session as part of the historical record of the group.

INSTRUCTIONS: To begin the activity your group will select a reporter to discuss the timeline in the report back session with the entire class. You will use your logs to review the work of the group and identify transition points where your group moved from one stage of group development to the next. Once your group has reached substantial agreement on the stages and the dates when the transitions occurred, the group members will create the timeline on the sheet of paper with markers, identifying the stages and dates when the group moved into each stage. Printing should be large and legible enough to be read across the room. Each group will affix their timeline to the classroom wall and, in turn, the reporters will describe the development of their task group with the class. Similarities and differences should be noted and discussed, taking into account the history and development of the class as a whole and the historical events that may have had an impact on the groups and members.

PRACTITIONER'S NOTES:

- At what stage(s) of group development would this activity be useful?

- How would member's characteristics, skills, and abilities influence the way you would modify and implement this activity?

- How would this activity contribute to the group goals, members' goals, and session goals?

· At what point in the group meeting would you introduce the activity?

· How would you evaluate the usefulness and impact of the activity on the group and its members?

ACTIVITY 5-14: Parting Gifts

IN THE CLASSROOM: This exercise will help the class to sum up your experiences and to look to future growth, emphasizing balance in approach to your professional practice.

IN THE FIELD: *Parting Gifts* is suitable for any age group as part of the separation phase. The gifts chosen should connect with some aspect of the group's experience together. For example, you could use bubble sets and bookmarks with relevant quotations or sayings to symbolize making time for both fun and more serious pursuits. You could put a bubble set and a bookmark in a lunch bag, decorating it with ribbon and labeling it with the recipient's name with colorful markers. With younger children's groups, bubble sets are often spilled. Homemade activity kits with art supplies or a light, bouncy toy might be good substitutes. In groups that have used horticultural activities, small plants (e.g., cut flowers, flowering annuals in spring, or cutting from houseplants in other seasons) can symbolize the need for caring and the potential for further growth. For groups where cost is an issue, members can use "found" items for purchased ones.

MATERIALS: Each class member will bring two inexpensive or "found" gifts to symbolize maintaining a balance in one's professional and private life.

GROUP SIZE: 12-15

TIME REQUIRED: 10 minutes.

SPACE REQUIREMENTS: Meeting room plus outdoor space for using the bubble sets.

PREPARATION: Purchase the supplies you will bring to the last class.

INSTRUCTIONS: When your turn comes, you will explain the symbolism of the gifts you have chosen. You will place your gifts in the designated spots, one for fun and one for more serious pursuits. When class members have each contributed their gifts, in turn you will each select one gift from the fun and serious collections to take with you to remember your experiences with the class.

PRACTITIONER'S NOTES:

·   With what types of groups would you use this activity?

·   At what stage(s) of group development would this activity be useful?

·   How would member's characteristics, skills, and abilities influence the way you would modify and implement this activity?

·   How would this activity contribute to the group goals, members' goals, and session goals?

· At what point in the group meeting would you introduce the activity?

· How would you evaluate the usefulness and impact of the activity on the group and its members?

Source: Contributed by Marcia Cohen, PhD, Professor, University of New England School of Social Work, Portland, ME.

APPENDIXES

Appendix A - *Classification of Activities by Type of Activity*

Type of Activity										
Arts & Crafts	4-2	4-3	4-17	5-2						
Conversation	3-2	3-7	3-12	6-4						
Discussion	1-4	3-10	3-11	3-16	4-4	4-11	4-13	5-3	6-1	7-4
Games	3-1	3-3	3-4	3-5	3-13	3-15	3-17	4-6	4-7	
Horticulture	4-3	4-17	5-1	6-4	6-5					
Movement	1-2	4-4	4-8							
Music	7-6	7-7	7-8	7-9	7-10					
Observation	1-1	3-14								
Pen/Paper	3-6	3-8	3-9	3-16	4-1	4-9	5-7	6-3	7-1	7-3	7-5
Photos	4-14	4-15	4-16							
Poetry	4-10									
Role Play	2-4	2-6	4-11	4-12	4-13	5-4				
Simulation	2-3	2-8	4-19	4-20	5-5	5-6	7-2			
Video	2-1	2-2	2-5	2-7	4-5	4-18	2-20			

Appendix B - *Classification of Activities by Stage of Group Development*

Preaffiliation	Power/Control	Intimacy	Differentiation	Separation
1-1	1-1	1-1	1-3	4-2
1-2	1-2	1-11	1-4	5-1
1-6	1-4	2-6	1-5	5-2
1-13	1-8	2-11	1-6	5-3
2-1	2-10	2-12	1-7	5-4
2-2	2-11	2-13	1-8	5-5
2-3	2-12	2-14	1-9	5-6
2-4	2-13	3-1	1-10	5-7
2-5	2-14	3-2	1-11	5-8
2-6	3-3	3-3	1-12	5-9
2-7	3-4	3-4	3-2	5-10
2-8	3-5	3-6	3-7	5-11
2-9	3-8	3-7	3-8	5-12
2-10	3-10	3-8	3-9	5-14
2-11	3-11	3-10	3-10	
2-12	4-3	3-11	3-11	
2-13	4-4	4-2	4-1	
2-14	4-5	4-5	4-2	
3-1	4-6	5-1	4-3	
3-2	4-7	5-2	4-4	
3-3	4-8	5-4	4-5	
3-5	4-9		4-6	
3-6	4-10		4-7	
4-2	4-11		4-8	
	4-12		4-9	
	4-13		4-10	
			4-11	
			4-12	
			4-13	
			4-14	
			4-15	

Garland, J.A., Jones, H.E., Kolodny, R.L. (1975). A model for stages of group development in social work groups (pp. 17-71). In S. Bernstein (Ed.). *Explorations in group work: Essays in theory and practice (Reprint).* Bloomfield, CT: Practitioner's Press.

Appendix C - *Classification of Activities by Type of Group: Task*

CLIENT NEED [*Team, Treatment Conference, Staff Development*]	ORGANIZATIONAL NEED [Committee, Cabinet, Board]	COMMUNITY NEED [Social Action, Coalition, Staff Development]
1-1 through 1-13		
2-1		2-1
2-2		
2-5		2-5
2-7		2-7
2-8	2-8	2-8
2-9		2-9
2-11	2-11	2-11
3-13		2-13
3-1		
3-2		
3-3		3-3
3-4		
3-7		
3-8		
3-9		
3-10		3-10
3-11	3-11	3-11
3-12	3-12	3-12
3-13	3-13	3-13
4-1		
4-2		
4-3	4-3	4-3
4-4 through 4-8	4-4 through 4-8	4-4 through 4-8
4-9		
4-10		
4-11 through 4-13	4-11 through 4-13	4-11 through 4-13
4-14		
5-1 through 5-14		5-1
		5-13

For explanation of task group categories, see Toseland, R.W. and Rivas, R.F. (2001). *An introduction to group work practice (4th ed.).* Boston: Allyn & Bacon, pp. 31-33. For additional discussion of group typologies, see also Zastrow, C. (2001). *Social work with groups (5th ed.).* Pacific Grove, CA: Brooks/Cole, pp. 4-11.

Appendix D - *Classification of Activities by Type of Group: Treatment*

Support	Educational	Growth	Therapy	Socialization
	1-1	1-1	1-1	
1-2	1-2	1-2		
	1-3	1-3		1-3
	1-6	1-6	1-6	1-6
1-7	1-7	1-7	1-7	1-7
1-8			1-8	1-8
1-11		1-11	1-11	1-11
1-13	1-13	1-13	1-13	1-13
2-1	2-1	2-1	2-1	2-1
2-2	2-2	2-2		2-2
2-3(C/T)	2-3(C/T)	2-3(C/T)	2-3(C/T)	2-3(C/T)
	2-4	2-4		
2-5	2-5	2-5		2-5
2-6(C/T)	2-6(C/T)	2-6(C/T)		2-6(C/T)
2-7	2-7	2-7		2-7
	2-8	2-8		
2-9	2-9	2-9	2-9	2-9
2-10		2-10	2-10	2-10
2-11	2-11	2-11	2-11	2-11
	2-12	2-12		
	2-13	2-13	2-13	2-13
2-14	2-14	2-14	2-14	2-14
3-1	3-1	3-1	3-1	3-1
3-2	3-2	3-2	3-2	3-2
	3-3	3-3		3-3
3-4	3-4	3-4	3-4	3-4
	3-5(C/T)	3-5(C/T)		3-5(C/T)
3-6	3-6	3-6		3-6
3-7		3-7	3-7	3-7
3-10	3-10	3-10	3-10	3-10
3-11	3-11	3-11	3-11	3-11
4-1	4-1	4-1	4-1	4-1
4-2		4-2		4-2
	4-3	4-3		4-3
	4-4	4-4		4-4
	5-5	4-5		4-5
	4-6	4-6		4-6
	4-7	4-7		4-7
	4-8	4-8		4-8
	4-11	4-11		4-11
	4-12	4-12		4-12
5-1 to 5-14	5-1 to 5-14	5-1 to 1-14	5-1 to 1-14	5-1 to 5-14

For explanation of task group categories, see Toseland, R.W. and Rivas, R.F. (2001). *An introduction to group work practice (4th ed.).* Boston: Allyn & Bacon, pp. 23. For additional discussion of group typologies, see also Zastrow, C. (2001). *Social work with groups (5th ed.).* Pacific Grove, CA: Brooks/Cole, pp. 4-11.

RESOURCE BIBLIOGRAPHY

Many web resources are listed below. However, due to the living nature of the Internet, you might find that some of these resources have moved or disappeared altogether. We have posted these URLs to our website where we can update them, if possible. Please visit our website at http://wadsworth.com/social_work_d/ .

Arts and Crafts

Art

Boyd, M.A. (1999). *The crafts supply source book: A comprehensive shop-by-mail guide for thousands of craft materials.* Cincinnati, OH: Betterway Books.

Fugaro, R.A. (1985). *A manual for sequential art activities for classified children and adolescents.* Springfield, IL: Charles C. Thomas.

Jennings, S. and Minde, A. (1993). *Art therapy and dramatherapy: Masks of the soul.* London: Jessica Kingsley Publishers.

Liebmann, M. (1986). *Art therapy for groups: A handbook of themes, games, and exercises.* Cambridge, MA: Brookline Books.

Makin, S.R. (2000). *Therapeutic art directives and resources: Activities and initiatives for individuals and groups.* London: Jessica Kingsley Publishers.

McMurray, J. (1990). *Creative arts with older people.* New York: Haworth Press.

Morris, N. (1984). *The lettering book.* Los Angeles: Price/Stern/Sloan.

Muller, B. (1987). *Painting with children.* Edinburgh, Scotland: Floris Books.

Perr, H. (1988). *Making art together step-by-step.* San Jose, CA: Resource Publications.

Post, H. and McTwigan, M. (1973). *Clay play.* Englewood Cliffs, NJ: Prentice-Hall.

Waller, D. (1993). *Group interactive art therapy: Its use in training and treatment.* London: Routledge.

On the Web: Art Therapy Resources

www.arttherapy.org [The American Art Therapy Association, Inc.]

home.ican.net/~phansen/pages/mainindex.html [Art Therapy in Canada]

Children's Crafts

Dahlstrom, C.F. (Ed.). (2001). *501 fun-to-make family crafts.* Des Moines, IA: Better Homes and Gardens Books.

Fiarotta, P. (1973). *Sticks & stones & ice cream cones.* New York: Workman.

Fiarotta, P. and Fiarotta, N. (1978). *Confetti: The kids' make-it-yourself, do-it-yourself party book.* New York: Workman.

Fitzjohn, S., Weston, M., and Large, J. (1993). *Festivals together: A guide to multi-cultural celebration.* Stroud, Gloucestershire: Hawthorne Press.

Frank, M. (1976). *I can make a rainbow.* Nashville, TN: Incentive Publications.

Greene, P.R. (1978). *Things to make.* New York: Random House.

Leaming, J. (1974). *Fun with string.* New York: Dover.

Lohf, S. (1987). *Things I can make with cloth*. San Francisco: Chronicle Books.

Pountney, K. (1977). *Creative crafts for children*. London: Faber and Faber.

Reyes, G. and Hindley, J. (1986). *Once there was a house and you can make it!* New York: Random House.

Schoemaker, K. (1978). *Creative Christmas: Simple crafts from many lands*. Minneapolis, MN: Winston Press.

Sunset Books (Eds.) (1977). *Children's crafts: Fun and creativity for ages 5-12*. Menlo Park, CA: Lane Publishing.

Wendorff, R. (1973). *How to make cornhusk dolls*. New York: Arco Publishing.

Zubrowski, B. (1981). *Messing around with drinking straw construction*. Boston: Little, Brown and Company.

Zubrowski, B. (1981). *Messing around with water pumps and siphons*. Boston: Little, Brown and Company.

Zubrowski, B. (1985). *Raceways: Having fun with balls and tracks*. New York: William Morrow and Company.

On the Web: Children's Crafts

www.abcbabysit.com

www.childrenfarandwide.com/childcrafts5.htm

www.hgtv.com

www.sitesforteachers.com

www.wtc-childrensmural.org

On the Web: Crafts Schools

www.penland.org

Knitting

Falick, M. (1998). *Kids knitting*. New York: Artisan.

Gosse, B. and Allerton, J. (1995). *A first book of knitting for children*. Gloucester, England: Wynstones Press.

Lydon, S.G. (1997). *The knitting sutra: Craft as spiritual practice*. San Francisco: Harper Collins.

Murphy, B. (2002). *Zen and the art of knitting: Exploring links between knitting, spirituality and creativity*. Avon, MA: Adams Media Corporation.

Myers, L.R. (2001). *The joy of knitting: Texture, color, design, and the global knitting circle*. Philadelphia: Running Press.

Von Wartburg, U. (1978). *The workshop book of knitting*. New York: Atheneum

On the Web: Knitting and Crocheting

www.maggiesrags.com/tips_children.htm

www.crochetpartners.org/Patterns.html

www.citiusa.com/paternsites.html

www.childrenincommon.org/project.html

countrywool.hypermart.net/knittingforneighborhoodl.htm

www.woolworks.org/patterns.html

Paper

D'Amato, J. and D'Amato, A. (1971). *Cardboard carpentry*. New York: The Lion Press.

Feliciano, K. (1999). *Making memory books by hand*. Gloucester, MA: Quarry Books.

Tremaine, J. (1997). *The step by step art of origami*. Godalming, Surrey, UK: Coombe Books.

Young, J. L. and Johnson, R.E. (2001). *The big idea book of heritage memories*. Escondido, CA: Primedia.

Quilting

Amor, J. (1991). *Flavor quilts for kids to make*. Paducah, KY: American Quilter's Society.

Hire, D.S. (Ed.) (2001). *Oxymorons: Absurdly logical quilts!* Paducah, KY: American Quilter's Society.

Kavaya, K. and Skemp, V. (2001). *Community quilts: How to organize, design, & make a group quilt*. Ashville, NC: Lark Books.

Weidman, M.L. (2001). *Quilted memories: Celebrations of life*. Lafayette, CA: C & TPublishing.

Spinning and Weaving

Castino, R. (1974). *Spinning and dyeing the natural way*. New York: Van Nostrand Reinhold.

dePaola, T. (1973). *Charlie needs a cloak*. New York: Simon & Schuster.

Lasky, K. (1980). *The weaver's gift*. New York: Frederick Warne.

Cooking with Children and Youth

Barrett, I. (1974). *Cooking is easy when you know how*. New York: Arco.

Baxter, K.M. (1978). *Come and get it: A natural foods cookbook for children*. Ann Arbor, MI: Children First Press.

Carey, D. and Large, J. (1982). *Festivals, families and food*. Stroud, England: Hawthorn Press.

Betty Crocker's cookbook for boys and girls. Racine, WI: Golden Books.

Johnson, J. (Ed.) (1985). *Kid's snacks*. Des Moines, IA: Better Homes and Gardens Books.

Kleven, E. (2001). *Sun bread*. New York: Dutton Children's Books.

KinderCare, Inc. (1984). *Half-pints in the kitchen*. Dallas, TX: Jokari/US.

Loo, M.B. (1978). *Meals of many lands: A cookbook for children*. Colorado Springs, CO: KitchenFare.

Pratt, D. (1998). *Let's stir it up! Kids' cookbook & earth friendly fun*. Salisbury Cove, ME: Harvest Hill Press.

On the Web: Cooking with Children

www.foodfunandfacts.com

www.childrenfarandwide.com/recipes.htm

Discussion Starters

Bolte, C. and McCusker, P. (1989). *Quick skits & discussion starters*. Loveland, CO: Group Books.

Carrel, S. (1993). *Group exercises for adolescents: A manual for therapists*. Newbury Park, CA: Sage.

Dossick, J. and Shea, E. (1988). *Creative therapy: 52 exercises for groups*. Sarasota, FL: Professional Resource Exchange.

Dossick, J. and Shea, E. (1990). *Creative therapy II: 52 more exercises for groups*. Sarasota, FL: Professional Resource Exchange.

Farnett, C., Forte, I, and Loss, B. (1989). *I've got me and I'm glad*. Nashville, TN: Incentive Publications.

Gochenour, T. (Ed.) (1993). *Beyond experience: The experiential approach to cross-cultural education (2nd ed.)*. Yarmouth, ME: Intercultural Press.

Lazarus, S. (1981). *The parenthood handbook: Thirty activities to teach adolescents about parenthood*. Menlo Park, CA: Addison-Wesley.

Moore, C.M. (1987). *Group techniques for idea building*. Newbury Park, CA: Sage.

Parry, A., Walker, M., and Heim, C. (1991). *Choosing non-violence: The Rainbow House handbook to a violence-free future for young children*. Chicago: Rainbow House/Arco Iris.

Pfeiffer, J.W. and Jones, J.E. (1979). *A handbook of structured experiences for human relations training*. LaJolla, CA: University Associates.

Schlenger, G.L. (1988). *Come and sit by me: Discussion programs for activity specialists*. Owings Mills, MD: National Health Publishing.

Simon, S.B., Howe, L.W. and Kirschenbaum, H. (1978). *Values clarification*. New York: A & W Publishers.

Storti, C. (1994). *Cross-cultural dialogues: 74 brief encounters with cultural difference*. Yarmouth, ME: Intercultural Press.

Thiagarajan, S. (1990). *Barnga: A simulation game on cultural clashes*. Yarmouth, ME: Intercultural Press.

Thiagarajan, S. (1995). *Diversity simulation games*. Amherst, MA: HRD Press.

Yaconelli, M. and Rice, W. (1979). *Super ideas for youth groups*. Grand Rapids, MI: Zondervan.

Yaconelli, M. and Rice, W. (1981). *Tension getters: 68 real-life problems and predicaments for today's youth*. Grand Rapids, MI: Zondervan.

On the Web: Tips for Discussion in Educational Groups

www.princeton.edu/~aiteachs/handbook/facilitating.html

www.vanderbilt.edu/cwp/leading.htm

curry.edschool.virginia.edu/go/multicultural/resources

www.redribbonworks.org [substance abuse prevention resources]

Games and Adventure-Based Activities

Brooking-Payne, K. (1996). *Games children play: How games and sport help children develop*. Stroud, Gloucestershire, UK: Hawthorn Press.

Dynes, R. (1990). *Creative games in groupwork*. Bicester, Oxford UK: Winslow Press.

Favour, E. (1974). *Bulletin X: Indian games, toys and pastimes of Maine and the Maritimes*. Bar Harbor, ME: The Robert Abbe Museum.

Fluegelman, A. (Ed.) (1976). *The new games book*. Garden City, NY: Doubleday.

Fluegelman, A. (Ed.) (1981). *More new games*. Garden City, NY: Doubleday.

Gass, M.A. (1993). *Adventure therapy: Therapeutic applications of adventure programming*. Dubuque, IA: Kendall/Hunt.

Gass, M.A. (1995). *Book of metaphors*. Dubuque, IA: Kendall/Hunt.

Harris, F.W. (1990). *Great games to play with groups*. Belmont, CA: Simon & Schuster Supplementary Education Group.

Hopson, D.P. (1996). *Juba this and Juba that: 100 African-American games for children*. New York: Simon & Schuster.

Kalman, B. (1995). *Games from long ago*. New York: Crabtree.

Lieberman, L.J. and Cowart, J.F. (1996). *Games for people with sensory impairments: Strategies for including individuals of all ages*. Champaign, IL: Human Kinetics.

Marcoux-Morris, S. (1998). *Game creations: Great physical education games for grades 4-9*. Durham, NC: Great Activities.

Marl, K. (1999). *The accessible games book*. London: Jessica Kingsley Publishers.

Michaelis, B. and O'Connel, J.M. (2000). *The game and play leader's handbook*. State College, PA: Venture.

Orlick, T. (1978). *The cooperative sports and games book: Challenge without competition*. New York: Pantheon.

Orlick, T. (1982). *The second cooperative sports and games book*. New York: Pantheon. Rohnke, K. (1985). *Silver bullets*. Iowa: Kendall/Hunt.

Rohnke, K. (1977). *Cowstails and cobras: A guide to ropes courses, initiative games, and other adventure activities*. Hamilton, MA: Project Adventure.

Rohnke, K. (1989). *Cowstails and cobras II: A guide to games, initiatives, ropes courses, and adventure curriculum*. Iowa: Kendall/Hunt.

Rohnke, K. and Butler, S. (1995). *Quicksilver: Adventure games, initiative problems, trust activities, and a guide to effective leadership*. Iowa: Kendall/Hunt.

Rohnke, K., Tait, C. and Wall, J. (1997). *The complete ropes course manual (2nd ed.)*. Dubuque, IA: Kendall/Hunt.

Searle, Y. and Streng, I. (1996). *The anti-bullying game*. Philadelphia: Jessica Kingsley Publishers.

Silberg, J. (1993). *Games to play with babies*. Beltsville, MD: Gryphon House.

Van Haren, W. and Kischnick, R. (1995). *Child's Play Parts 1 & 2*. Stroud, Gloucestershire UK: Hawthorn Press.

Wilkins, J. (2001). *Group activities to inlcude students with special needs: Developing social interactive skills*. Thousand Oaks, CA: Corwin Press.

Wilner, I. (2000). *The baby's game book*. New York: Greenwillow Books.

On the Web: Adventure-Based Activities

www.curricstudies.edu.ubc.ca/wcourses/Pete/tcpa.html [Outdoor education resources]

www.geocities.com/ti...ecreation_Therapy_and_Activity_Links.html

www.jccn.iowa-city/ia/us~recdsab1/LITActivity.htm

fdsa.gcsu.edu:6060/lgillis/AT/front.htm

General Activities

Borba, M. and Borba, C. (1978). *Self-esteem: A classroom affair*. San Francisco: Harper & Row.

Caney, S. (1975). *Play book*. New York: Workman.

Carey, D. and Large, J. (1982). *Festivals, families and food*. Stroud, England: Hawthorn Press.

Cooper, S., Frynes-Clinton, C. and Rowling, M. (1986). *The children's year*. Stroud, U.K.: Hawthorne Press.

Elliott, J.A. and Elliott, J.E. (1999). *Recreation for older adults: Individual and group activities*. State College, PA: Venture.

Hanks, J. (Ed.) (2001). *The outrageously big activity, play and project book*. London: Hermes House.

Hansen, K. (Ed.) (1986). *Great ideas from "Learning" Vols. 1-3*. Springhouse, PA: Springhouse.

Hass, C.B. (1987). *Look at me: Creative learning activities for babies and toddlers*. Chicago: Chicago Review Press.

Lear, R. (1996). *Play helps: Toys and activities for children with special needs (4th ed.)*. Oxford, UK: Butterworth-Heinemann.

Marzollo, J. and Lloyd, J. (1974). *Learning through play*. New York: Harper & Row. McManus, R. and Jennings, G. (Eds.) (1996). *Structured exercises for promoting family and group strengths*. New York: Haworth Press.

Plummer, D. (2001). *Helping children to build self-esteem: A photocopiable activities book.* Philadelphia: Jessica Kingsley Publishers.

Rappaport Morris, L. and Shulz, L. (1989). *Creative play activities for children with disabilities: A resource book for teachers and parents (2nd ed.).* Champaign, IL: Human Kinetics Books.

Remocker, A.J. and Storch, E.T. (1987). *Action speaks louder: A handbook of structured group techniques (4th ed.).* Edinburgh, Scotland: Churchill Livingstone.

Smith, S. (1982). *Echoes of a dream: Creative beginnings for parent and child.* London, Ontario, Canada: Waldorf School Association of London.

Stumbo, N.J. (1998). *Leisure education IV: Activities for individuals with substance addictions.* State College, PA: Venture.

Thomson, J. (1994). *Natural childhood.* New York: Simon & Schuster.

Vance, E.G. (1974). *The everything book.* Racine, WI: Western Publishing.

Warner, P. (1999). *Baby play & learn.* Minnetonka, MN: Meadowbrook Press.

Wiseman, A.S. (1997). *Making things: The handbook of creative discovery.* Boston: Little, Brown and Company.

On the Web: General Activities

www.seniorservices.ca/directories.php?area=113

discoveryschool.com

On the Web: Therapeutic Activities

www.therapeuticresources.com/sampleactivity.html

www.rider.edu/users/suler/inclassex.html

Journaling and Bibliotherapy

Jones, E.H. (2001). *Bibliotherapy for bereaved children: Healing reading.* Philadelphia: Jessica Kingsley Publishers.

On the Web: Journaling

www.sdcoe.k12.ca.us/score/actbank/tjournal.htm [Journaling activities with school age children]

cradleofbones.tripod.com/paper/id9.html [Visual Journals and Paper Arts]

On the Web: Bibliotherapy

indiana.edu/~eric_rec/ieo/digests/d82.html [Bibliotherapy overview]

Movement Activities

Champion, A. (1990). *Earth mazes.* Emeryville, CA: Bacchus Press.

Clements, C.B. (1994). *The arts/fitness Quality of Life activities program: Creative ideas for working with older adults in group settings.* Baltimore: Health Professions Press.

Cole, J. (1989). *Anna Banana: 101 jump rope rhymes*. New York: Morrow Junior Books.

Halprin, A. (2000). *Dance as a healing art: Returning to health with movement and imagery*. Mendocino, CA: LifeRhythm Books.

Levy, F.J. (Ed.). (1995). *Dance and other expressive therapies: When words are not enough*. New York: Routledge.

Payne, H. (Ed.) (1992). *Dance movement therapy: Theory and practice*. London: Tavistock/Routledge.

Rooyackers, P. (1996). *101 dance games for children: Fun and creativity with movement*. Alameda, CA: Hunter House.

Sands, H.R. (2001). *The healing labyrinth*. Hauppauge, NY: Barron's Educational Series.

Torbert, M. (1980). *Follow me: A handbook of movement activities for children*. New York: Prentice-Hall.

Weikart, P.S. (1997). *Movement plus rhymes, songs, and singing games: Activities for young children*. Ypsilanti, MI: High/Scope Press.

On the Web: Dance Therapy

www.adta.org [American Dance Therapy Association]

www.admt.org.uk [Association for Dance Movement Therapy UK]

On the Web: Dance and Music Resources

www.cdss.org [Country Dance and Song Society]

www.izaak.unh.edu/hnhtmd/sandfree.htm [Sandy Freedman Collection of folk dance resources]

On the Web: Labyrinths

www.labyrinthproject.com [General information on labyrinth projects in the US]

www.mcli.dist.maricopa.edu/smc/labyrinth/ [A labyrinth project at South Mountain Community College]

math.sunysb.edu/~tony/mazes/juniordemo.html [An activity to use with children]

Music

Blood, P. and Patterson, A. (Eds.) (1992). *Rise up singing: The group singing songbook*. Bethlehem, PA: A Sing Out Publication.

Boni, M.B. (Ed.) (1947). *Fireside book of folk songs*. New York: Simon and Schuster.

Deaver. M.J. (1975). *Sound and silence: Developmental learning for children through music*. Pikeville, KY: Curriculum Development and Research.

Groetzinger, I. and Gode, M. (1958). *Play and sing: Hayes action song book for kindergarten and primary*. Wilkinsburg, PA: Hayes School Publishing.

Jenkins, E. (1966). *The Ella Jenkins song book for children*. New York: Oak Publications.

Lebret, E. (1971). *Pentatonic songs for nursery, kindergarten and grades I and II*. North Vancouver, Canada: Steiner Book Center.

Nordoff, P. and Robbins, C. (1972). *Therapy in music for handicapped children*. New York: St. Martin's Press.

Plach, T. (1980). *The creative use of music in group therapy*. Springfield, IL: Charles C. Thomas, Publisher.

Roos, A. and White, A. (1968). *Brownies' own songbook*. New York: Roos & Coe-White Associates.

Schalkwijk, F.W. (1994). *Music and people with developmental disabilities: Music therapy, remedial music making, and musical activities*. London: Jessica Kingsley Publishers.

Schulberg, C.H. (1981). *The music therapy sourcebook: A collection of activities categorized and analysed*. New York: Human Sciences Press.

Standley, J. (1991). *Music techniques in therapy, counseling, and special education*. St. Louis, MO: MMB Music.

On the Web: Music Therapy

www.musictherapy.org [American Music Therapy Association]

www.musictherapy.ca [Canadian Music Therapy Association]

Nature and Environment

Allison, L. (1977). *The Sierra Club summer book*. New York: Wings Books.

Berger, T. (1992). *The harvest craft book*. Edinburgh, Scotland: Floris Books.

Boy Scouts of America. (1978). *Boy Scout Fieldbook*. New York: Workman.

Bradley, C. and Fitzsimons, C. (1999). *Outdoor activities for kids*. New York: Lorenz Books.

Consalvo, C.M. (1996). *Changing pace: Outdoor games for experiential learning*. Amherst, MA: HRD Press.

Hewson, M. (1994). *Horticulture as therapy*. Guelph, Ontario: Greenmor Printing.

Kraul, W. (1989). *Earth, water, fire and air: Playful explorations in the four elements*. Edinburgh, Scotland: Floris Books.

Lohf, S. (1990). *Nature crafts*. Chicago: Children's Press.

Lovejoy, S. (1999). *Roots, shoots, buckets and boots*. New York: Workman.

Leeuwen, M. and Moeskops. J. (1990). *The nature corner*. Edinburgh, Scotland: Floris Books.

Malone, J.S. (1999). *Wild adventures: A guidebook of activities for building connections with others and the earth*. Needham Heights, MA: Simon & Schuster.

McDonald, E. (1976). *Plants as therapy*. New York: Praeger Publishers.

Minter, S. (1995). *The healing garden*. Boston: Charles E. Tuttle.

Petrash, C. (1992). *Earthways: Simple environmental activities for young children*. Mt. Rainier, MD: Gryphon House, Inc.

Relf, D. (Ed.) (1992). *The role of horticulture in human well-being and social development*.

Portland, OR: Timber Press.

Reynolds, R.A. (1995). *Bring me an ocean: Nature as teacher, messenger, and   intermediary.* Acton, MA: VanderWyk & Burnham.

Rights, M. (1981). *Beastly neighbors.* Boston: Little, Brown and Company.

Rhoades, D. (1995). *Garden crafts for kids: 50 great reasons to get your hands dirty.*

New York: Sterling Publishing.

Richardson, B. (1998). *Gardening with children.* Newtown, CT: The Taunton Press.

On the Web: Farm Experiential Education

www.farmschool.org

On the Web: Horticultural Therapy Resources

www.umit.maine.edu/~elin_mackinnon/ELINM1.html (Horticultural Therapy Methods   class at University of Maine School of Social Work)

www.ahta.org (American Horticultural Therapy Association)

www.chta.ca (Canadian Horticultural Therapy Association)

www.cityfarmer.org/hortherp70.html

Photography

Weiser, J. (1993). *Phototherapy techniques: Exploring the secrets of personal snapshots and family albums.* San Francisco: Jossey-Bass.

Wick, W. & Marzollo, J. (1999). *I spy treasure hunt: A book of picture riddles.* New York: Scholastic Books.

On the Web: Photo Therapy Resources

www.phototherapy-centre.com/home.htm

www.seniorservices.ca/directories.php?area=118

www.kporterfield.com/healing/photography.html

Storytelling and Drama

Aliki, (1984). *Feelings.* New York: Mulberry Books.

Bany-Winters, L. (1997). *On stage: Theater games and activities for kids.* Chicago: Chicago Review Press.

Children's Community Service Department. (1977*). Ring a ring o' roses.* Flint, MI: Flint Board of Education.

Crimmens, P. (1998). *Storymaking and creative groupwork with older people.* Philadelphia: Jessica Kingsley Publishers.

Gersie, A. (1997). *Reflections on therapeutic story making: The use of stories in groups.* Philadelphia: Jessica Kingsley Publishers.

Gwynne, F. (1976). *A chocolate moose for dinner.* New York: E. P. Dutton.

Mellon, N. (1992). *The art of storytelling.* Boston: Element Books.

Mellon, N. (2000). *Storytelling with children.* Stroud, Gloucestershire, UK: Hawthorne Press.

Newton, B. (1999). *Improvisation: Use what you know—make up what you don't (2nd ed.).* Scottsdale, AZ: Gifted Psychology Press.

Scieszka, J. (1989). *The true story of the 3 little pigs! By A. Wolf.* New York: Viking.

Seeger, P. and Jacobs, P.D. (2000). *Pete Seeger's storytelling book.* San Diego: Harcourt.

ssipsis (1990). *Molly Molasses and me: A collection of living adventures.* Brooks, ME: Little Letterpress Robin Hood Books.

Stangl, J. (1982). *Paper stories.* Belmont, CA: Pitman Learning.

Trelease, J. (2001). *The read-aloud handbook.* New York: Penguin Books.

Zimmerman, E. (1983). *Shadow puppets for children.* Edinburgh, Scotland: Floris Books.

On the Web: Reading Resources

www.mainepbs.org/agoodread/bryan.html

www.trelease-on-reading.com

Team and Community Building

Adams, B. (2001). *The everything leadership book.* Holbrook, MA: Adams Media Corp.

Anderson, T. (1991). *The reflecting team: Dialogues and dialogues about the dialogues.* New York: W.W. Norton.

Barlow, C.A., Blythe, J.A., and Edmonds, M. (1999). *A handbook of interactive exercises for groups.* Boston: Allyn and Bacon.

Bendaly, L. (1996). *Games teams play: Dynamic activities for tapping team potential.* Toronto: McGraw-Hill Ryerson.

Consalvo, C.M. (1993). *Experiential training activities for outside and in.* Amherst, MA: HRD Press.

Epstein, R. (1996). *Creativity games for trainers.* New York: Training McGraw-Hill.

Forbess-Greene, S. (1983). *The encyclopedia of icebreakers: Structured activities that warm-up, motivate, challenge, acquaint and energize.* San Diego, CA: Applied Skills Press.

Lee, B. and Balkwill, M. (1996). *Participatory planning for action.* Toronto: Commonact Press.

Manning, G., Curtis, K., and McMillan, S. (1996). *Building community: The human side of work.* Duluth, MN: Whole Person Associates.

Nilson, C. (1993). *Team games for trainers.* New York: McGraw-Hill.

Powers, R.B. (1999). *An alien among us: A diversity game.* Yarmouth, ME: Intercultural Press.

Scannell, E. E. and Newstrom, J.W. (1994). *Still more games trainers play.* New York:McGraw-Hill.

Scannell, E.E. and Newstrom, J.W. (1998). *The big book of presentation games.* New York: McGraw-Hill.

Steinberg, A. and Stephen, D. (1999). *City works: Exploring your community.* New York: The New Press.

Thiagarajan, S. (1994). *Cash games: Exploring interpersonal concepts and skills.* Amherst, MA: HRD Press.

Thiagarajan, S. (1994). *SH! Sexual harassment simulation.* Amherst, MA: HRD Press.

Thiagarajan, S. (1994). *Teamwork games: Exploring factors that affect a team's performance.* Amherst, MA: HRD Press.

Thiagarajan, S. (1994). *Triangles: Exploring organizational relationships.* Amherst, MA: HRD Press.

Thiagarajan, S. (1996). *Creativity games: Eliminate problems and profit from opportunities.* Amherst, MA: HRD Press.

Thiagarajan, S. and Thiagarajan, R. (1995). *More cash games: Exploring interpersonal principles and procedures.* Amherst, MA: HRD Press.

Ukens, L. (1997). *Getting together: Icebreakers and energizers.* San Francisco: Jossey-Bass/Pfeiffer.

West, E. (1997). *201 icebreakers, group mixers, warmups, energizers, and playful activities.* New York: McGraw-Hill.

Wiener, R. (1997). *Sociodrama and team-building.* Philadelphia: Jessica Kingsley Publishers.

On the Web: Community Work

www.community-work-training.org.uk [Community Work Training Company]

On the Web: Icebreakers

www.hcc.hawaii.edu/intranet/committees/FacDevCom/guidebk/teachtip/namegame.html

www.hcc.hawaii.edu/intranet/committees/FacDevCom/guidebk/teachtip/pigprofi.html

On the Web: Brainstorming

www.geocities.com/CollegePark/Union/2106/circle.html

On the Web: Team Learning

www.geocities.com/CollegePark/Union/2106/team.html

Toy Making

Berger. P. (1994). *Feltcraft: Making dolls, gifts and toys.* Edinburgh, Scotland: Floris Books.

Blocksma, M. and Blocksma, D. (1985). *Easy-to-make water toys that really work.* Englewood Cliffs, NJ: Prentice-Hall.

Burns, E. (1990). *Hanky-panky: Traditional handkerchief toys.* Aptos, CA: Elizabeth Burns.

Gorge, A.A. (1970). *Creative toymaking.* London: Ward Lock.

Jaffke, F. (1981). *Doll making*. Edinburgh, Scotland: Floris Books.

Joseph, J. (1972). *Folk toys around the world and how to make them*. New York: Parents Magazine Press.

Lohf, S. (1989). *Building your own toys*. Chicago: Children's Press.

Pack-o-Fun. (1967). *How to make sock toys*. Park Ridge, IL: Clapper Publishing.

Videos

Coleman, L. (Producer) & Porter, D. (Director). (1993). *Mattering, A Journey with Rural Youth* [Motion Picture]. (Available from Edmund S. Muskie Institute of Public Affairs, University of Southern Maine, 207-780-4430).

Cacoyannis, M. (Producer & Director). (1964). *Zorba the Greek* [Motion Picture]. (Available from Magnetic Video, Industrial Park, Farmington Hills, MI 48204).

DeVito, D., Shamberg, M., & Sher, S. (Producers) & Soderbergh, S. (Director) (2000). *Erin Brokovich* [Motion Picture]. (Available from from MCA Home Video, Inc., Universal City Plaza, Universal City, CA 91608).

Knight, C.W. (Producer) & Zeiff, H. (Director) (1989). *The Dream Team* [Motion Picture]. (Available from MCA Home Video, 70 Universal City Plaza, Universal City, CA 91608).

Marx, F., James, S., & Gilbert, P. (Producers) and James, S. (Director). (1994). *Hoop Dreams* [Motion Picture]. (Available from New Line Home Video, Turner Home Entertainment).

Simpson, D. & Bruckheimer, J. (Producers) and Smith, J.M. (Director). (no date). *Dangerous Minds* [Motion Picture]. (Available from Buena Vista Home Video, Dept. CS, Burbank, CA 91521).

Swords, T., Victor, D.J., & Styler, T. (Producers) and Hershman, J. (Director). (2001). Greenfingers *[Motion Picture]. (Available from Columbia Tri-Star Home Entertainment, 10202 W. Washington Blvd. Culver City, CA 90232-3195).*

Tanen, N. & Hughes, J. (Producers) & Hughes, J. (Writer/Director). (1985). The Breakfast Club *[Motion Picture]. (Available from MCA Home Video, Inc., 10 Universal City Plaza, Universal City, CA 91608).*

Topping, J. (Producer) & Thomas, B. (Director). (2000). *28 Days* [Motion Picture]. (Available from Columbia TriStar Home Video, 10202 W. Washington, Blvd, Culver City CA 90232-3195).

Zaentz, S. & Douglas, M. (Producers) and Forman, M. (Director). (1975). *One Flew Over the Cuckoo's Nest* [Motion Picture]. (Available from Warner Home Video, 4000 Warner Blvd., Burbank, CA 91422).

Zieff, H. (Director). (1989). *The Dream Team* [Motion Picture]. (Available from Universal Studios Home Video).

Tapes

Children of Selma. (1987). *Who will speak for the children.* Cambridge, MA: Rounder Records.

Cook, B. and Ramey, S. (1987). Soliloquy. *Carousel.* Universal City, CA: MCA Records.

Columbia Treasury of the American Musical Theatre. (1973). America. *West side story.* New York: Columbia Records

Columbia Treasury of the American Musical Theatre. (1973). Gee, Officer Krupke. *West side story.* New York: Columbia Records.

Rodgers & Hammerstein (1958). Carefully taught. *South Pacific.* New York: RCA/Ariola International.

Seeger, P. (2000). *American folk, game & activity songs.* Washington, DC: Smithsonian Folkway Recordings.

Seeger, P., Sapp, J., and Kahn, S. (1986). Black, Brown and White Blues. *Carry it on.* Chicago: Flying Fish Records, Inc.

Seeger, P., Sapp, J., and Kahn, S. (1986). I'd Rather Be An Engineer. *Carry it on.* Chicago: Flying Fish Records, Inc.

RESOURCE LOCATIONS FOR BOOKS AND MATERIALS

Catalog companies

Child Craft, P.O. Box 29149, Mission, KS 66201-9149, 1-800-631-5657

Childs Work Childs Play, Center for Applied Psychology, 441N. 5th St., 3rd Fl., Phildelphia, PA 19123-4011

Eddie Bowers Publishing, Inc., 2600 Jackson Street, Dubuque, IA 52001-3342 [physical education, recreation, health, dance]

Family Pastimes, RR#4, Perth, Ontario, Canada K7H 3C6

Hearth Song, P.O. Box B, Sebastopol, CA 95473-0601 1-800-325-2502 [children's toys & crafts]

J & A Handy-Crafts, Inc., 165 S. Pennsylvania Ave., Lindenhurst, NY 11757

Kids Rights, 10100 Park Cedar Drive, Charlotte, NC 28210, 1-800-892-KIDS

Mar*Co Products, Inc., Dept. F2001, 1443 Old York Rd., Warminster, PA 1897 1-800-448-2197 [games, puppets, books, videos, manuals for professionals working with children]

McBer & Company, Training Resources Group, 116 Huntington Ave., Boston, MA 02116 (617) 437-7080 [LSI Self Scoring Inventory and Interpretation Booklet]

Music for Little People, Box 1460, Redway, CA 95560, 1-800-346-4445

Nature Watch, P.O. Box 1668, Reseda, CA 91337

Pfeiffer, Games & Activities: Training Solutions for Today's HRD Professionals, 350 Sansome St., 5th Fl., San Francisco, CA 94204

School-Age NOTES, P.O. Box 40205. Nashville, TN 37204, 1-800-410-8780 [after school resources]

Search Institute, The Banks Building, 615 First Avenue NE, Suite 125, Minneapolis, MN 55413-2211 [resources to support youth work in communities]

T.C. Timber Habermaass Corporation, P.O. Box 42, Skaneateles, NY 13152 [t.c. timber toys and blocks]

Toys to Grow On, P.O. Box 17, Long Beach, Ca 90801

Local Resources

Craft and specialty craft shops (e.g., weaving workshops, knitting supply stores)

Educational bookstores, sometimes called "teacher's stores"

Party stores for inexpensive craft supplies

Children's museums for programming and resources

Children's librarian for books on specific topics for discussion (i.e., new sibling, moving, starting at a new school, divorce, death)

National Association for Education of Young Children and their local chapters hold conferences where suppliers display craft and activity resources.

On the Web

Abilitations: www2.abilitations.com [exercise resources for persons with special needs]

Activity Based Supplies: www.absupplies.com [Roman and catenary arch kits]

Association for Play Therapy: www.a4pt.org

At-Risk Resources: www.at-risk.com

Canadian Play Therapy Institute: www.playtherapy.org

Childcraft: www/chimetime.com [early childhood resources]

Crayola Company: www.crayola.com

E.C.E. Supply Ltd.: www.ecesupply.com [teaching resources and supplies]

Edmund Scientific: www.scientificsonline.com [Roman arch kits]

Frank Lloyd Wright Preservation Trust: www.wrightcatalog.org [nature pattern blocks]

Jist Life: www.jistlife.com [books, manuals, videos, and counseling resources]

Lakeshore Learning Materials: www.lakershorelearning.com

Mar*Co: www.marcoproducts.com [therapeutic activity books and supplies for children and youth]

Oriental Trading Company, Inc.: www.orientaltrading.com [inexpensive party supplies]

School-Age NOTES: www.AfterSchoolCatalog.com

Sandtastik, Inc: www.sandtastik.com [colored sand and related play therapy resources]

Summit Learning: www.summitlearning.com [catenary and Roman arch kits]

Teachers Center: www.teacherscenter.com

Teachers Planet Superstore of Educational Supplies: www.teachersplanet.com

Therapeutic Recreation Store: www.recreationtherapy.com

Toys of the Trade: Toytrade@yahoo.com [play therapy resources]

Wellness Reproductions & Publishing, LLC: www.wellness-resources.com

TEXTS WITH CONTENT ON USE OF ACTIVITIES IN GROUP WORK

Alissi, A.S. (Ed.) (1980). *Perspectives on social group work practice: A book of readings.* New York: The Free Press.

Alissi, A.S. and Corto Mergins, C.G. (1997). *Voices from the field: Group work responds.* New York: The Haworth Press.

Bernstein, S. (Ed.) (1973). *Explorations in group work: Essays in theory and practice.*

   Boston, MA: Milford House.

Brandler, S. and Roman, C. (1991). *Group work: Skills and strategies for effective interventions.* New York: The Haworth Press.

Brooks-Harris, J.E. and Stock-Ward, S. R. (1999). *Workshops: Designing and facilitating experiential learning.* Thousand Oaks, CA: Sage.

Burnside, I. (1986). *Working with the elderly: Group process and techniques (2nd ed.)* Boston: Jones and Bartlett Publishers.

Chesner, A. and Hahn, H. (2001). *Creative advances in groupwork.* Philadelphia: Jessica Kingsley Publishers.

Corey, M.S. and Corey, G. (2002). *Groups: Process and practice, 6th ed.* Pacific Grove,CA: Brooks/ Cole.

Coyle, G. L. (Ed.) (1937). *Studies in group behavior.* New York: Harper & Brothers. Coyle, G. L. (1947). *Group experience and democratic values.* New York: The Woman's Press.

Doel, M. and Sawdon, C. (1999). *The essential groupworker: Teaching and learning creative group work.* London: Jessica Kingsley Publishers.

Doel, M. and Shardlow, S. (1998). *The new social work practice: Exercises and activities for training and developing social workers.* Brookfield, VT: Ashgate Publishing.

Dwivedi, K. N. (Ed.) (1993). *Group work with children and adolescents: A handbook.* London: Jessica Kingsley Publishers.

Foster, P.M. (Ed.) (1983). *Activities and the "well elderly."* New York: The Haworth Press.

Garvin, C.D. (1997). *Contemporary group work. (3rd ed.).* Boston: Allyn and Bacon.

Gass, M.A. (Ed.) (1993). *Adventure therapy: Therapeutic applications of adventure programming.* Dubuque, IA: Kendall/Hunt.

Gladding, S.T. (1995). *Group work: A counseling specialty (2nd ed.).* Englewood Cliffs, NJ: Prentice-Hall.

Glassman, U. and Kates, L. (1990). *Group work: A humanistic approach.* Newbury Park, CA: Sage.

Goldstein, H. (2001). *Experiential learning: A foundation for social work education and practice.* Alexandria, VA: Council on Social Work Education.

Greif, G.L. and Ephross, P.H. (1997). *Group work with populations at risk.* New York: Oxford University Press.

Hartford, M. (1972). *Groups in social work.* Itasca, IL: Peacock Publications.

Henry, S. (1992). *Group skills in social work: A four-dimensional approach (2nd ed.).* Pacific Grove, CA: Brooks/Cole

Henry, S., East, J., and Schmitz, C. (Eds.) (2002). *Social work with groups: Mining the gold.* New York: The Haworth Press.

Horwood, B. (Ed.) (1995). *Experience and the curriculum.* Dubuque, IA: Kendall/Hunt.

Itin, C.M. (Ed.) (1998). *Exploring the boundaries of adventure therapy: International perspectives.* Boulder, CO: Association for Experiential Education.

Jacobs, E.E., Masson, R.L., and Harvill, R.L. (2002). *Group counseling strategies and skills (4th ed.).* Pacific Grove, CA: Brooks/Cole.

Jennings, S. and Minde, A. (1993). *Art therapy and dramatherapy: Masks of the soul.* London: Jessica Kingsley Publishers.

Johnson, D.W. and Johnson, F.P. (1997). *Joining together: Group theory and group skills (6th ed.).* Boston: Allyn & Bacon.

Johnson, J. (1977). *Use of groups in schools.* Lanham, MD: University Press of America.

Johnson, L.C. (1995). *Social work practice: A generalist approach (5th ed.).* Boston: Allyn and Bacon.

Kraft, R.J. and Kielsmeirer, J. (Eds.) (1995). *Experiential learning in schools and highereducation.* Boulder, CO: Association for Experiential Education.

Kolodny, R.L. and Garland, J.A. (Eds.) (1984). *Group work with children and adolescents.* New York: The Haworth Press.

Konopka, G. (1963). *Social group work: A helping process.* Englewood Cliffs, NJ: Prentice Hall.

Kormanski, C. (1999). *The team: Explorations in group process.* Denver: Love Publishing.

Kurland, R. and Salmon, R. (1998). *Teaching a methods course in social work with groups.* Alexandria, VA: Council on Social Work Education.

Kurland, R. and Salmon, R. (1995). *Group work practice in a troubled society: Problems and opportunities.* New York: The Haworth Press.

Malekoff, A. (1997). *Group work with adolescents: Principles and practice.* New York: The Guildford Press.

Mesbur, E. and Jacobs, J. (1989). *Understanding and working with groups.* Toronto, Ontario: School of Social Work, Ryerson Polytechnic University.

Middleman, R.R. (1980). *The non-verbal method in working with groups.* Hartford, CT: Practitioners Press.

Columbia University PressMiddleman, R.R. (Ed.) (1983). *Activities and action in groupwork*. New York: The Haworth Press.

Middleman, R.R. and Goldberg, G.W. (1990). *Skills for direct practice in social work*. New York: Columbia University Press.

Northen, H. (1969). *Social work with groups*. New York: Columbia University Press.

Pack-Brown, S.P., Whittington-Clark, L.E., and Parker, W.M. (1998). *Images of me: A guide to group work with African-American women*. Boston: Allyn and Bacon.

Pernell, R. B. (Ed.) (1998). *A training program for leadership of youth groups*. Cleveland, OH: The Northeast Ohio Chapter, Association for the Advancement of Social Work with Groups.

Ramey, J.H. (1995). *Bibliography on group work*. Akron, OH: Association for the Advancement of Social Work with Groups.

Redl, F. (1966). *When we deal with children*. New York: The Free Press.

Rose, S.D. and Edleson, J.L. (1988). *Working with children and adolescents in groups*. San Francisco: Jossey-Bass.

Rubin, J.A. (Ed.) (1987). *Approaches to art therapy: Theory and technique*. New York: Brunner/Mazel.

Schwartz, W. and Zalba, S. R. (Eds.) (1971). *The practice of group work*. New York: Columbia University Press.

Shulman, L. (1999). *The skills of helping individuals, families, and groups (4th ed.)*. Itasca, IL: Peacock.

Simon, P. (Ed.) (1971). *Play and game theory in group work: A collection of papers by Neva Leona Boyd*. Chicago: University of Illinois at Chicago.

Stanford, G. (1977). *Developing effective classroom groups: A practical guide for teachers*. New York: Hart Publishing.

Sugerman, D., Doherty, K.L., and Garvey, D.E., Gass, M.A. (2000). *Reflective learning: Theory and practice*. Dubuque, IA: Kendall/Hunt.

Sullivan, D. F. (1952). *Readings in group work*. New York: Association Press.

Sundel, M., Glasser, P., Sarri, R., and Vinter, R. (1985). *Individual change through small groups (2nd ed.)*. New York: The Free Press.

Toseland, R.W. and Rivas, R.F. (1998). *An introduction to group work practice (3rd ed.)*. Boston: Allyn and Bacon.

Vernell, B. (1994). *Understanding and using groups*. London: Whiting and Birch.

Waller, D. (1993). *Group interactive art therapy: Its use in training and treatment*. London: Routledge.

Wilson, G. and Ryland, G. (1949). *Social group work practice: The creative use of the social process*. Hebron, CT: Practitioner's Press.

Zastrow, C. (2001). *Social work with groups: Using the class as a group leadership laboratory*. Pacific Grove, CA: Brooks/Cole.

ARTICLES WITH CONTENT ON USE OF ACTIVITIES IN GROUP WORK

Abels, P. and Abels, S.L. (1990). The basic game. *Social Work with Groups, 13*(4), 23-126.

Adams, M. (1987). The use of ritual. *The Journal of Experiential Education, 10*(3), 36-37.

Alvarez, A.R. (2002). Pitfalls, pratfalls, shortfalls, and windfalls: Reflections on forming and being formed by groups. In R. Kurland and A. Malekoff (Eds.). *Stories celebrating group work: It's not always easy to sit on your mouth.* New York: The Haworth Social Work Practice Press.

Alvarez, A.R. and Cabbil, L.M. (2001). The MELD Program: Promoting personal change and social justice through a year-long multicultural group experience. *Social Work with Groups, 24*(1), 3-20.

Anderson, J. D. (1985). Working with groups: Little-known facts that challenge well-known myths. *Small Group Behavior, 16*(3), 267-283.

Bitel, M.C. (1999). Mixing up the goulash: Essential ingredients in the "art" of social group work. *Social Work with Groups, 22*(2/3), 77-99.

Brouillette, L. (1992). Using drama as a cultural bridge. *The Journal of Experiential Education 15*(3), 41-45.

Cohen, M.B. and DeLois, K. (2001). Training in tandem: Co-facilitation and role modeling in a group work course. *Social Work with Groups, 24*(1), 21-36.

Collins, L. (1998). How do you spell hippopotamus: The use of group work in after-school tutoring programs. *Social Work with Groups, 21*(1/2), 61-75.

Compton, V. (1997). Hot metal/hot words: Event and interpretation as development tools in adolescent self-concept. *The Journal of Experiential Education, 20*(2), 94-101.

Duffy, T.K. (1994). The check-in and other go-rounds in group work: Guidelines for use. *Social Work with Groups, 17*(1/2), 163-175.

Dutton, S.E. (2001). Urban youth development—Broadway style: Using theatre and group work as vehicles for positive youth development. *Social Work with Group, 16*(3), 39-58.

Ewert, A. (1992). Group development through experiential education: Does it happen? *The Journal of Experiential Education, 15*(2), 56.

Fatout, M. F. (1993). Physically abused children: Activity as a therapeutic medium. *Social Work with Group, 16*(3), 83-96.

Gerber, M. (1998). Winning isn't everything: A group work approach to sports teams. *Social Work with Groups, (21)*3, 35-48.

Greenberg, N. (1988). Teaching problem solving through group discussion of fictional stories. *The Journal of Experiential Education, 11*(3), 27-30.

Griffith, S.C. (1990). Cooperative learning techniques in the classroom. *The Journal of Experiential Education, 13*(2), 41-44.

Halperin, D. (2001). The play's the thing: How social group work and theatre transformed a group into a community. *Social Work with Groups, 24*(2), 27-46.

Hammel, H. (1986). How to design a debriefing session. *The Journal of Experiential Education, 9*(3), 20-25.

Haslett, D.C. (1998). The education task group: Teaching proposal writing to social work students. *Social Work with Groups, 20*(4), 55-67.

Hill, C.O. and Relf, P.D. Gardening as an outdoor activity in geriatric institutions. *Activities, Adaptations and Aging, 3*(1), 47-54.

Jackson, K. (2002). Therapeutic art and recreation: Healing through self-expression. *Social Work Today, 2*(9), 8-11.

Jordan, D. (1990). Snips and snails and puppy dog tails...The use of gender free language in experiential education. *The Journal of Experiential Education, 13*(2), 45-49.

Jones, A.T. (1992). Mask making: The use of the expressive arts in leadership development. *The Journal of Experiential Education, 15*(1), 28-34.

Kaplan, C. (2001). The purposeful use of performance in groups: A new look at the balance of task and process. *Social Work with Groups, 24*(2), 47-67.

Katz, S. (1988). Photocollage as a therapeutic modality for working with groups. *Social Work with Groups, 10*(4), 83-90.

Leonard, L.S. (1990). Storytelling as experiential education *The Journal of Experiential Education, 13*(2), 12-17.

Leonard, L.S. (1991). Storytelling tips for experiential educators. *The Journal of Experiential Education, 14*(1), 45-46.

Lopez, J. (1991). Group work as a protective factor for immigrant youth. *Social Work with Groups, 14*(1), 29-40.

Lynn, M. and Nisivoccia, D. (1995). Activity-oriented group work: Enhancing socialization. *Social Work with Groups, 18*(2/3), 95-106.

Lyons, S.M. (2000). Make, make, make some music: Social group work with mothers and babies, too. *Social Work with Groups, 23*(2), 37-54.

MacKinnon, E. (2001). Sowing the healing seeds of horticultural therapy. *Social Work Today,* November 26, 17-19.

MacLennan, B.W. (1994). Groups for poorly socialized children in the elementary school. *Journal of Child and Adolescent Group Therapy, 4*(4), 243-250.

Malekoff, A. (2002). The power of group work with kids: Lessons learned. In R. Kurland and A. Malekoff (Eds.). *Stories celebrating group work: It's not always easy to sit on your mouth.* New York: The Haworth Social Work Practice Press.

Marsiglia, F.F. (2002). Navigating in groups...Experiencing the cultural as political. In R. Kurland and A. Malekoff (Eds.). *Stories celebrating group work: It's not always easy to sit on your mouth.* New York: The Haworth Social Work Practice Press.

Mazza, N. (2002). Social work and poetry: Two arts beat as one. *Social Work Today, 2*(9), 14-17.

Miller, J. and Donner, S. (2000). More than just talk: The use of racial dialogues to combat racism. *Social Work with Groups, 23*(1), 31-53.

Miller, R. (2002). Will the real healer please take a bow. In R. Kurland and A. Malekoff (Eds.). *Stories celebrating group work: It's not always easy to sit on your mouth.* New York: The Haworth Social Work Practice Press.

Newman, E.W. (2002). Bell choir, somersaults, and cucumber sandwiches: A journey in understanding the importance of positive group norms. In R. Kurland and A. Malekoff (Eds.). *Stories celebrating group work: It's not always easy to sit on your mouth.* New York: The Haworth Social Work Practice Press.

Perchick, M. (1992). Rehabilitation through photography: The power of photography as physical and emotional therapy. *Photographic Society of America Journal, 58*(12), 13.

Perschbacher, R. (1984). An application of reminiscence in an activity setting. *The Gerontologist, 24*(4), 343-345.

Pollio, D.E. (1995). Hoops group: Group work with young "street" men. *Social Work with Groups, 18*(2/3), 107-122.

Porter, T. (1999). Beyond metaphor: Applying a new paradigm of change to experiential debriefing. *The Journal of Experiential Education, 22*(2), 85-90.

Potocky, M. (1993). An art therapy group for clients with chronic schizophrenia. *Social Work with Groups, 16*(3), 73-82.

Racine, G. and Sevigny, O. (2001). Changing the rules: A board game lets homeless women tell their stories. *Social Work with Groups, 23*(4), 25-38.

Rawe, A. (2002 May/June). A dream conferred: Ashley Bryan leads kids across cultural bridges with his rousing gospel of poetry and art. *Hope Magazine,* (31), 12-15.

Relf, D. (1982). Horticulture: A therapeutic tool. *Journal of Rehabilitation, 39*(1), 27-29.

Relf, P.D. (1990). The use of horticulture in vocational rehabilitation. *Journal of Rehabilitation, 47*(3), 53-56.

Renner, P. (1990). Games to train by. *Training and Development Journal (January),* 22-30.

Reynolds, F.C. (1990). Mentoring artistic adolescents through expressive therapy. *The Clearinghouse. 64,* (November/December), 83-86.

Rittner, B. and Nakanishi, M. (1993). Challenging stereotypes and cultural biases through small group process. *Social Work with Groups, 16*(4), 5-23.

Roberts, N.S. and Drogin, E.B. (1993). The outdoor recreation experience: Factors affecting participation of African American women. *The Journal of Experiential Education, 16*(1), 14-18.

Salmons-Rue, J. (1990). Interactive theatre as a dramatic resource. *The Journal of Experiential Education, 1*(2), 54-55.

Schnekenburger, E. (1995). Waking the heart up: A writing group's story. *Social Work with Groups, (18)*4, 19-40.

Steiner, S., Stromwall, L.K., Brzuzy, S. and Gerdes, K. (1999). Using cooperative learning strategies in social work education. *Journal of Social Work Education, 35*(2), 253-264.

Thompson, M.E. (1993). Building groups on students' knowledge and experience. *Teaching Sociology, 21*(1), 95-99.

Umbrell, T.W. (2002, May/June). Learning off the land. *Hope Magazine,* (31), 28-31.

Upitis, R. (1989). Building an arts playground. *The Journal of Experiential Education, 12*(2), 22-27.

Vinter, R.D. (1967). Program activities: An analysis of their effect on participant behavior. In R.D. Vinter (Ed.) *Readings in group work practice.* Ann Arbor, MI: Campus Publishers.

Waite, L.M. (1993). Drama therapy in small groups with the developmentally disabled. *Social Work with Groups, 16*(4), 95-108.

Walsh, R., Richardson, M.A. and Cardey, R.M. (1991). Structured fantasy approaches to children's group therapy. *Social Work with Groups, 14*(1), 57-73.

Warren, K. (1988). Teaching consensus decision making. *The Journal of Experiential Education, 11*(3), 38-39.

Wolfe, L.A. and Collins-Wolfe, J.A. (1983). Action techniques for therapy with famiilies with young children. *Family Relations (January),* 81-87.

Wright, W. (2002). But I want to do a *real* group: A personal journey from snubbing to loving, to theorizing to demanding activity-based group work. In R. Kurland and A. Malekoff (Eds.). *Stories celebrating group work: It's not always easy to sit on your mouth.* New York: The Haworth Social Work Practice Press.

Wright, W. (1999). The use of purpose in on-going activity groups: A framework maximizing the therapeutic impact. *Social Work with Groups, 22*(2/3), 31-54.

Wyatt, S. (1997). Dialogue, reflection, and community. *The Journal of Experiential Education, 20*(2), 80-84.